C-632   CAREER EXAMINATION SERIES

This is your
PASSBOOK for...

Public Health Nutritionist

Test Preparation Study Guide
Questions & Answers

NATIONAL LEARNING CORPORATION®

COPYRIGHT NOTICE

This book is SOLELY intended for, is sold ONLY to, and its use is RESTRICTED to individual, bona fide applicants or candidates who qualify by virtue of having seriously filed applications for appropriate license, certificate, professional and/or promotional advancement, higher school matriculation, scholarship, or other legitimate requirements of education and/or governmental authorities.

This book is NOT intended for use, class instruction, tutoring, training, duplication, copying, reprinting, excerption, or adaptation, etc., by:

1) Other publishers
2) Proprietors and/or Instructors of "Coaching" and/or Preparatory Courses
3) Personnel and/or Training Divisions of commercial, industrial, and governmental organizations
4) Schools, colleges, or universities and/or their departments and staffs, including teachers and other personnel
5) Testing Agencies or Bureaus
6) Study groups which seek by the purchase of a single volume to copy and/or duplicate and/or adapt this material for use by the group as a whole without having purchased individual volumes for each of the members of the group
7) Et al.

Such persons would be in violation of appropriate Federal and State statutes.

PROVISION OF LICENSING AGREEMENTS – Recognized educational, commercial, industrial, and governmental institutions and organizations, and others legitimately engaged in educational pursuits, including training, testing, and measurement activities, may address request for a licensing agreement to the copyright owners, who will determine whether, and under what conditions, including fees and charges, the materials in this book may be used them. In other words, a licensing facility exists for the legitimate use of the material in this book on other than an individual basis. However, it is asseverated and affirmed here that the material in this book CANNOT be used without the receipt of the express permission of such a licensing agreement from the Publishers. Inquiries re licensing should be addressed to the company, attention rights and permissions department.

All rights reserved, including the right of reproduction in whole or in part, in any form or by any means, electronic or mechanical, including photocopying, recording, or by any information storage and retrieval system, without permission in writing from the Publisher.

Copyright © 2024 by
National Learning Corporation

212 Michael Drive, Syosset, NY 11791
(516) 921-8888 • www.passbooks.com
E-mail: info@passbooks.com

PUBLISHED IN THE UNITED STATES OF AMERICA

PASSBOOK® SERIES

THE *PASSBOOK® SERIES* has been created to prepare applicants and candidates for the ultimate academic battlefield – the examination room.

At some time in our lives, each and every one of us may be required to take an examination – for validation, matriculation, admission, qualification, registration, certification, or licensure.

Based on the assumption that every applicant or candidate has met the basic formal educational standards, has taken the required number of courses, and read the necessary texts, the *PASSBOOK® SERIES* furnishes the one special preparation which may assure passing with confidence, instead of failing with insecurity. Examination questions – together with answers – are furnished as the basic vehicle for study so that the mysteries of the examination and its compounding difficulties may be eliminated or diminished by a sure method.

This book is meant to help you pass your examination provided that you qualify and are serious in your objective.

The entire field is reviewed through the huge store of content information which is succinctly presented through a provocative and challenging approach – the question-and-answer method.

A climate of success is established by furnishing the correct answers at the end of each test.

You soon learn to recognize types of questions, forms of questions, and patterns of questioning. You may even begin to anticipate expected outcomes.

You perceive that many questions are repeated or adapted so that you can gain acute insights, which may enable you to score many sure points.

You learn how to confront new questions, or types of questions, and to attack them confidently and work out the correct answers.

You note objectives and emphases, and recognize pitfalls and dangers, so that you may make positive educational adjustments.

Moreover, you are kept fully informed in relation to new concepts, methods, practices, and directions in the field.

You discover that you are actually taking the examination all the time: you are preparing for the examination by "taking" an examination, not by reading extraneous and/or supererogatory textbooks.

In short, this PASSBOOK®, used directedly, should be an important factor in helping you to pass your test.

PUBLIC HEALTH NUTRITIONIST

DUTIES
Assists in the conduct of a public health nutrition program; performs related duties as required.

SCOPE OF THE EXAMINATION
Written test designed to test for knowledge, skills, and/or abilities in such areas as:
1. Concepts of nutrition and dietetics;
2. Principles of nutrition education;
3. Advising and interacting with others; and
4. Preparing written material.

HOW TO TAKE A TEST

I. YOU MUST PASS AN EXAMINATION

A. WHAT EVERY CANDIDATE SHOULD KNOW

Examination applicants often ask us for help in preparing for the written test. What can I study in advance? What kinds of questions will be asked? How will the test be given? How will the papers be graded?

As an applicant for a civil service examination, you may be wondering about some of these things. Our purpose here is to suggest effective methods of advance study and to describe civil service examinations.

Your chances for success on this examination can be increased if you know how to prepare. Those "pre-examination jitters" can be reduced if you know what to expect. You can even experience an adventure in good citizenship if you know why civil service exams are given.

B. WHY ARE CIVIL SERVICE EXAMINATIONS GIVEN?

Civil service examinations are important to you in two ways. As a citizen, you want public jobs filled by employees who know how to do their work. As a job seeker, you want a fair chance to compete for that job on an equal footing with other candidates. The best-known means of accomplishing this two-fold goal is the competitive examination.

Exams are widely publicized throughout the nation. They may be administered for jobs in federal, state, city, municipal, town or village governments or agencies.

Any citizen may apply, with some limitations, such as the age or residence of applicants. Your experience and education may be reviewed to see whether you meet the requirements for the particular examination. When these requirements exist, they are reasonable and applied consistently to all applicants. Thus, a competitive examination may cause you some uneasiness now, but it is your privilege and safeguard.

C. HOW ARE CIVIL SERVICE EXAMS DEVELOPED?

Examinations are carefully written by trained technicians who are specialists in the field known as "psychological measurement," in consultation with recognized authorities in the field of work that the test will cover. These experts recommend the subject matter areas or skills to be tested; only those knowledges or skills important to your success on the job are included. The most reliable books and source materials available are used as references. Together, the experts and technicians judge the difficulty level of the questions.

Test technicians know how to phrase questions so that the problem is clearly stated. Their ethics do not permit "trick" or "catch" questions. Questions may have been tried out on sample groups, or subjected to statistical analysis, to determine their usefulness.

Written tests are often used in combination with performance tests, ratings of training and experience, and oral interviews. All of these measures combine to form the best-known means of finding the right person for the right job.

II. HOW TO PASS THE WRITTEN TEST

A. NATURE OF THE EXAMINATION

To prepare intelligently for civil service examinations, you should know how they differ from school examinations you have taken. In school you were assigned certain definite pages to read or subjects to cover. The examination questions were quite detailed and usually emphasized memory. Civil service exams, on the other hand, try to discover your present ability to perform the duties of a position, plus your potentiality to learn these duties. In other words, a civil service exam attempts to predict how successful you will be. Questions cover such a broad area that they cannot be as minute and detailed as school exam questions.

In the public service similar kinds of work, or positions, are grouped together in one "class." This process is known as *position-classification*. All the positions in a class are paid according to the salary range for that class. One class title covers all of these positions, and they are all tested by the same examination.

B. FOUR BASIC STEPS

1) Study the announcement

How, then, can you know what subjects to study? Our best answer is: "Learn as much as possible about the class of positions for which you've applied." The exam will test the knowledge, skills and abilities needed to do the work.

Your most valuable source of information about the position you want is the official exam announcement. This announcement lists the training and experience qualifications. Check these standards and apply only if you come reasonably close to meeting them.

The brief description of the position in the examination announcement offers some clues to the subjects which will be tested. Think about the job itself. Review the duties in your mind. Can you perform them, or are there some in which you are rusty? Fill in the blank spots in your preparation.

Many jurisdictions preview the written test in the exam announcement by including a section called "Knowledge and Abilities Required," "Scope of the Examination," or some similar heading. Here you will find out specifically what fields will be tested.

2) Review your own background

Once you learn in general what the position is all about, and what you need to know to do the work, ask yourself which subjects you already know fairly well and which need improvement. You may wonder whether to concentrate on improving your strong areas or on building some background in your fields of weakness. When the announcement has specified "some knowledge" or "considerable knowledge," or has used adjectives like "beginning principles of…" or "advanced … methods," you can get a clue as to the number and difficulty of questions to be asked in any given field. More questions, and hence broader coverage, would be included for those subjects which are more important in the work. Now weigh your strengths and weaknesses against the job requirements and prepare accordingly.

3) Determine the level of the position

Another way to tell how intensively you should prepare is to understand the level of the job for which you are applying. Is it the entering level? In other words, is this the position in which beginners in a field of work are hired? Or is it an intermediate or advanced level? Sometimes this is indicated by such words as "Junior" or "Senior" in the class title. Other jurisdictions use Roman numerals to designate the level – Clerk I, Clerk II, for example. The word "Supervisor" sometimes appears in the title. If the level is not indicated by the title, check the description of duties. Will you be working under very close supervision, or will you have responsibility for independent decisions in this work?

4) Choose appropriate study materials

Now that you know the subjects to be examined and the relative amount of each subject to be covered, you can choose suitable study materials. For beginning level jobs, or even advanced ones, if you have a pronounced weakness in some aspect of your training, read a modern, standard textbook in that field. Be sure it is up to date and has general coverage. Such books are normally available at your library, and the librarian will be glad to help you locate one. For entry-level positions, questions of appropriate difficulty are chosen — neither highly advanced questions, nor those too simple. Such questions require careful thought but not advanced training.

If the position for which you are applying is technical or advanced, you will read more advanced, specialized material. If you are already familiar with the basic principles of your field, elementary textbooks would waste your time. Concentrate on advanced textbooks and technical periodicals. Think through the concepts and review difficult problems in your field.

These are all general sources. You can get more ideas on your own initiative, following these leads. For example, training manuals and publications of the government agency which employs workers in your field can be useful, particularly for technical and professional positions. A letter or visit to the government department involved may result in more specific study suggestions, and certainly will provide you with a more definite idea of the exact nature of the position you are seeking.

III. KINDS OF TESTS

Tests are used for purposes other than measuring knowledge and ability to perform specified duties. For some positions, it is equally important to test ability to make adjustments to new situations or to profit from training. In others, basic mental abilities not dependent on information are essential. Questions which test these things may not appear as pertinent to the duties of the position as those which test for knowledge and information. Yet they are often highly important parts of a fair examination. For very general questions, it is almost impossible to help you direct your study efforts. What we can do is to point out some of the more common of these general abilities needed in public service positions and describe some typical questions.

1) General information

Broad, general information has been found useful for predicting job success in some kinds of work. This is tested in a variety of ways, from vocabulary lists to questions about current events. Basic background in some field of work, such as sociology or economics, may be sampled in a group of questions. Often these are principles which have become familiar to most persons through exposure rather than through formal training. It is difficult to advise you how to study for these questions; being alert to the world around you is our best suggestion.

2) Verbal ability

An example of an ability needed in many positions is verbal or language ability. Verbal ability is, in brief, the ability to use and understand words. Vocabulary and grammar tests are typical measures of this ability. Reading comprehension or paragraph interpretation questions are common in many kinds of civil service tests. You are given a paragraph of written material and asked to find its central meaning.

3) Numerical ability

Number skills can be tested by the familiar arithmetic problem, by checking paired lists of numbers to see which are alike and which are different, or by interpreting charts and graphs. In the latter test, a graph may be printed in the test booklet which you are asked to use as the basis for answering questions.

4) Observation

A popular test for law-enforcement positions is the observation test. A picture is shown to you for several minutes, then taken away. Questions about the picture test your ability to observe both details and larger elements.

5) Following directions

In many positions in the public service, the employee must be able to carry out written instructions dependably and accurately. You may be given a chart with several columns, each column listing a variety of information. The questions require you to carry out directions involving the information given in the chart.

6) Skills and aptitudes

Performance tests effectively measure some manual skills and aptitudes. When the skill is one in which you are trained, such as typing or shorthand, you can practice. These tests are often very much like those given in business school or high school courses. For many of the other skills and aptitudes, however, no short-time preparation can be made. Skills and abilities natural to you or that you have developed throughout your lifetime are being tested.

Many of the general questions just described provide all the data needed to answer the questions and ask you to use your reasoning ability to find the answers. Your best preparation for these tests, as well as for tests of facts and ideas, is to be at your physical and mental best. You, no doubt, have your own methods of getting into an exam-taking mood and keeping "in shape." The next section lists some ideas on this subject.

IV. KINDS OF QUESTIONS

Only rarely is the "essay" question, which you answer in narrative form, used in civil service tests. Civil service tests are usually of the short-answer type. Full instructions for answering these questions will be given to you at the examination. But in case this is your first experience with short-answer questions and separate answer sheets, here is what you need to know:

1) Multiple-choice Questions

Most popular of the short-answer questions is the "multiple choice" or "best answer" question. It can be used, for example, to test for factual knowledge, ability to solve problems or judgment in meeting situations found at work.

A multiple-choice question is normally one of three types—
- It can begin with an incomplete statement followed by several possible endings. You are to find the one ending which *best* completes the statement, although some of the others may not be entirely wrong.
- It can also be a complete statement in the form of a question which is answered by choosing one of the statements listed.

- It can be in the form of a problem – again you select the best answer.

Here is an example of a multiple-choice question with a discussion which should give you some clues as to the method for choosing the right answer:

When an employee has a complaint about his assignment, the action which will *best* help him overcome his difficulty is to
    A. discuss his difficulty with his coworkers
    B. take the problem to the head of the organization
    C. take the problem to the person who gave him the assignment
    D. say nothing to anyone about his complaint

In answering this question, you should study each of the choices to find which is best. Consider choice "A" – Certainly an employee may discuss his complaint with fellow employees, but no change or improvement can result, and the complaint remains unresolved. Choice "B" is a poor choice since the head of the organization probably does not know what assignment you have been given, and taking your problem to him is known as "going over the head" of the supervisor. The supervisor, or person who made the assignment, is the person who can clarify it or correct any injustice. Choice "C" is, therefore, correct. To say nothing, as in choice "D," is unwise. Supervisors have and interest in knowing the problems employees are facing, and the employee is seeking a solution to his problem.

2) True/False Questions

The "true/false" or "right/wrong" form of question is sometimes used. Here a complete statement is given. Your job is to decide whether the statement is right or wrong.

SAMPLE: A roaming cell-phone call to a nearby city costs less than a non-roaming call to a distant city.

This statement is wrong, or false, since roaming calls are more expensive.

This is not a complete list of all possible question forms, although most of the others are variations of these common types. You will always get complete directions for answering questions. Be sure you understand *how* to mark your answers – ask questions until you do.

V. RECORDING YOUR ANSWERS

Computer terminals are used more and more today for many different kinds of exams.

For an examination with very few applicants, you may be told to record your answers in the test booklet itself. Separate answer sheets are much more common. If this separate answer sheet is to be scored by machine – and this is often the case – it is highly important that you mark your answers correctly in order to get credit.

An electronic scoring machine is often used in civil service offices because of the speed with which papers can be scored. Machine-scored answer sheets must be marked with a pencil, which will be given to you. This pencil has a high graphite content which responds to the electronic scoring machine. As a matter of fact, stray dots may register as answers, so do not let your pencil rest on the answer sheet while you are pondering the correct answer. Also, if your pencil lead breaks or is otherwise defective, ask for another.

Since the answer sheet will be dropped in a slot in the scoring machine, be careful not to bend the corners or get the paper crumpled.

The answer sheet normally has five vertical columns of numbers, with 30 numbers to a column. These numbers correspond to the question numbers in your test booklet. After each number, going across the page are four or five pairs of dotted lines. These short dotted lines have small letters or numbers above them. The first two pairs may also have a "T" or "F" above the letters. This indicates that the first two pairs only are to be used if the questions are of the true-false type. If the questions are multiple choice, disregard the "T" and "F" and pay attention only to the small letters or numbers.

Answer your questions in the manner of the sample that follows:

32. The largest city in the United States is
    A. Washington, D.C.
    B. New York City
    C. Chicago
    D. Detroit
    E. San Francisco

1) Choose the answer you think is best. (New York City is the largest, so "B" is correct.)
2) Find the row of dotted lines numbered the same as the question you are answering. (Find row number 32)
3) Find the pair of dotted lines corresponding to the answer. (Find the pair of lines under the mark "B.")
4) Make a solid black mark between the dotted lines.

VI. BEFORE THE TEST

Common sense will help you find procedures to follow to get ready for an examination. Too many of us, however, overlook these sensible measures. Indeed, nervousness and fatigue have been found to be the most serious reasons why applicants fail to do their best on civil service tests. Here is a list of reminders:

- Begin your preparation early – Don't wait until the last minute to go scurrying around for books and materials or to find out what the position is all about.
- Prepare continuously – An hour a night for a week is better than an all-night cram session. This has been definitely established. What is more, a night a week for a month will return better dividends than crowding your study into a shorter period of time.
- Locate the place of the exam – You have been sent a notice telling you when and where to report for the examination. If the location is in a different town or otherwise unfamiliar to you, it would be well to inquire the best route and learn something about the building.
- Relax the night before the test – Allow your mind to rest. Do not study at all that night. Plan some mild recreation or diversion; then go to bed early and get a good night's sleep.
- Get up early enough to make a leisurely trip to the place for the test – This way unforeseen events, traffic snarls, unfamiliar buildings, etc. will not upset you.
- Dress comfortably – A written test is not a fashion show. You will be known by number and not by name, so wear something comfortable.

- Leave excess paraphernalia at home – Shopping bags and odd bundles will get in your way. You need bring only the items mentioned in the official notice you received; usually everything you need is provided. Do not bring reference books to the exam. They will only confuse those last minutes and be taken away from you when in the test room.
- Arrive somewhat ahead of time – If because of transportation schedules you must get there very early, bring a newspaper or magazine to take your mind off yourself while waiting.
- Locate the examination room – When you have found the proper room, you will be directed to the seat or part of the room where you will sit. Sometimes you are given a sheet of instructions to read while you are waiting. Do not fill out any forms until you are told to do so; just read them and be prepared.
- Relax and prepare to listen to the instructions
- If you have any physical problem that may keep you from doing your best, be sure to tell the test administrator. If you are sick or in poor health, you really cannot do your best on the exam. You can come back and take the test some other time.

VII. AT THE TEST

The day of the test is here and you have the test booklet in your hand. The temptation to get going is very strong. Caution! There is more to success than knowing the right answers. You must know how to identify your papers and understand variations in the type of short-answer question used in this particular examination. Follow these suggestions for maximum results from your efforts:

1) Cooperate with the monitor

The test administrator has a duty to create a situation in which you can be as much at ease as possible. He will give instructions, tell you when to begin, check to see that you are marking your answer sheet correctly, and so on. He is not there to guard you, although he will see that your competitors do not take unfair advantage. He wants to help you do your best.

2) Listen to all instructions

Don't jump the gun! Wait until you understand all directions. In most civil service tests you get more time than you need to answer the questions. So don't be in a hurry. Read each word of instructions until you clearly understand the meaning. Study the examples, listen to all announcements and follow directions. Ask questions if you do not understand what to do.

3) Identify your papers

Civil service exams are usually identified by number only. You will be assigned a number; you must not put your name on your test papers. Be sure to copy your number correctly. Since more than one exam may be given, copy your exact examination title.

4) Plan your time

Unless you are told that a test is a "speed" or "rate of work" test, speed itself is usually not important. Time enough to answer all the questions will be provided, but this does not mean that you have all day. An overall time limit has been set. Divide the total time (in minutes) by the number of questions to determine the approximate time you have for each question.

5) Do not linger over difficult questions

If you come across a difficult question, mark it with a paper clip (useful to have along) and come back to it when you have been through the booklet. One caution if you do this – be sure to skip a number on your answer sheet as well. Check often to be sure that you have not lost your place and that you are marking in the row numbered the same as the question you are answering.

6) Read the questions

Be sure you know what the question asks! Many capable people are unsuccessful because they failed to *read* the questions correctly.

7) Answer all questions

Unless you have been instructed that a penalty will be deducted for incorrect answers, it is better to guess than to omit a question.

8) Speed tests

It is often better NOT to guess on speed tests. It has been found that on timed tests people are tempted to spend the last few seconds before time is called in marking answers at random – without even reading them – in the hope of picking up a few extra points. To discourage this practice, the instructions may warn you that your score will be "corrected" for guessing. That is, a penalty will be applied. The incorrect answers will be deducted from the correct ones, or some other penalty formula will be used.

9) Review your answers

If you finish before time is called, go back to the questions you guessed or omitted to give them further thought. Review other answers if you have time.

10) Return your test materials

If you are ready to leave before others have finished or time is called, take ALL your materials to the monitor and leave quietly. Never take any test material with you. The monitor can discover whose papers are not complete, and taking a test booklet may be grounds for disqualification.

VIII. EXAMINATION TECHNIQUES

1) Read the general instructions carefully. These are usually printed on the first page of the exam booklet. As a rule, these instructions refer to the timing of the examination; the fact that you should not start work until the signal and must stop work at a signal, etc. If there are any *special* instructions, such as a choice of questions to be answered, make sure that you note this instruction carefully.

2) When you are ready to start work on the examination, that is as soon as the signal has been given, read the instructions to each question booklet, underline any key words or phrases, such as *least, best, outline, describe* and the like. In this way you will tend to answer as requested rather than discover on reviewing your paper that you *listed without describing*, that you selected the *worst* choice rather than the *best* choice, etc.

3) If the examination is of the objective or multiple-choice type – that is, each question will also give a series of possible answers: A, B, C or D, and you are called upon to select the best answer and write the letter next to that answer on your answer paper – it is advisable to start answering each question in turn. There may be anywhere from 50 to 100 such questions in the three or four hours allotted and you can see how much time would be taken if you read through all the questions before beginning to answer any. Furthermore, if you come across a question or group of questions which you know would be difficult to answer, it would undoubtedly affect your handling of all the other questions.

4) If the examination is of the essay type and contains but a few questions, it is a moot point as to whether you should read all the questions before starting to answer any one. Of course, if you are given a choice – say five out of seven and the like – then it is essential to read all the questions so you can eliminate the two that are most difficult. If, however, you are asked to answer all the questions, there may be danger in trying to answer the easiest one first because you may find that you will spend too much time on it. The best technique is to answer the first question, then proceed to the second, etc.

5) Time your answers. Before the exam begins, write down the time it started, then add the time allowed for the examination and write down the time it must be completed, then divide the time available somewhat as follows:
   - If 3-1/2 hours are allowed, that would be 210 minutes. If you have 80 objective-type questions, that would be an average of 2-1/2 minutes per question. Allow yourself no more than 2 minutes per question, or a total of 160 minutes, which will permit about 50 minutes to review.
   - If for the time allotment of 210 minutes there are 7 essay questions to answer, that would average about 30 minutes a question. Give yourself only 25 minutes per question so that you have about 35 minutes to review.

6) The most important instruction is to *read each question* and make sure you know what is wanted. The second most important instruction is to *time yourself properly* so that you answer every question. The third most important instruction is to *answer every question*. Guess if you have to but include something for each question. Remember that you will receive no credit for a blank and will probably receive some credit if you write something in answer to an essay question. If you guess a letter – say "B" for a multiple-choice question – you may have guessed right. If you leave a blank as an answer to a multiple-choice question, the examiners may respect your feelings but it will not add a point to your score. Some exams may penalize you for wrong answers, so in such cases *only*, you may not want to guess unless you have some basis for your answer.

7) Suggestions
   a. Objective-type questions
      1. Examine the question booklet for proper sequence of pages and questions
      2. Read all instructions carefully
      3. Skip any question which seems too difficult; return to it after all other questions have been answered
      4. Apportion your time properly; do not spend too much time on any single question or group of questions

5. Note and underline key words – *all, most, fewest, least, best, worst, same, opposite*, etc.
6. Pay particular attention to negatives
7. Note unusual option, e.g., unduly long, short, complex, different or similar in content to the body of the question
8. Observe the use of "hedging" words – *probably, may, most likely,* etc.
9. Make sure that your answer is put next to the same number as the question
10. Do not second-guess unless you have good reason to believe the second answer is definitely more correct
11. Cross out original answer if you decide another answer is more accurate; do not erase until you are ready to hand your paper in
12. Answer all questions; guess unless instructed otherwise
13. Leave time for review

b. Essay questions
1. Read each question carefully
2. Determine exactly what is wanted. Underline key words or phrases.
3. Decide on outline or paragraph answer
4. Include many different points and elements unless asked to develop any one or two points or elements
5. Show impartiality by giving pros and cons unless directed to select one side only
6. Make and write down any assumptions you find necessary to answer the questions
7. Watch your English, grammar, punctuation and choice of words
8. Time your answers; don't crowd material

8) Answering the essay question

Most essay questions can be answered by framing the specific response around several key words or ideas. Here are a few such key words or ideas:

M's: manpower, materials, methods, money, management
P's: purpose, program, policy, plan, procedure, practice, problems, pitfalls, personnel, public relations

a. Six basic steps in handling problems:
1. Preliminary plan and background development
2. Collect information, data and facts
3. Analyze and interpret information, data and facts
4. Analyze and develop solutions as well as make recommendations
5. Prepare report and sell recommendations
6. Install recommendations and follow up effectiveness

b. Pitfalls to avoid
1. *Taking things for granted* – A statement of the situation does not necessarily imply that each of the elements is necessarily true; for example, a complaint may be invalid and biased so that all that can be taken for granted is that a complaint has been registered

2. *Considering only one side of a situation* – Wherever possible, indicate several alternatives and then point out the reasons you selected the best one
3. *Failing to indicate follow up* – Whenever your answer indicates action on your part, make certain that you will take proper follow-up action to see how successful your recommendations, procedures or actions turn out to be
4. *Taking too long in answering any single question* – Remember to time your answers properly

IX. AFTER THE TEST

Scoring procedures differ in detail among civil service jurisdictions although the general principles are the same. Whether the papers are hand-scored or graded by machine we have described, they are nearly always graded by number. That is, the person who marks the paper knows only the number – never the name – of the applicant. Not until all the papers have been graded will they be matched with names. If other tests, such as training and experience or oral interview ratings have been given, scores will be combined. Different parts of the examination usually have different weights. For example, the written test might count 60 percent of the final grade, and a rating of training and experience 40 percent. In many jurisdictions, veterans will have a certain number of points added to their grades.

After the final grade has been determined, the names are placed in grade order and an eligible list is established. There are various methods for resolving ties between those who get the same final grade – probably the most common is to place first the name of the person whose application was received first. Job offers are made from the eligible list in the order the names appear on it. You will be notified of your grade and your rank as soon as all these computations have been made. This will be done as rapidly as possible.

People who are found to meet the requirements in the announcement are called "eligibles." Their names are put on a list of eligible candidates. An eligible's chances of getting a job depend on how high he stands on this list and how fast agencies are filling jobs from the list.

When a job is to be filled from a list of eligibles, the agency asks for the names of people on the list of eligibles for that job. When the civil service commission receives this request, it sends to the agency the names of the three people highest on this list. Or, if the job to be filled has specialized requirements, the office sends the agency the names of the top three persons who meet these requirements from the general list.

The appointing officer makes a choice from among the three people whose names were sent to him. If the selected person accepts the appointment, the names of the others are put back on the list to be considered for future openings.

That is the rule in hiring from all kinds of eligible lists, whether they are for typist, carpenter, chemist, or something else. For every vacancy, the appointing officer has his choice of any one of the top three eligibles on the list. This explains why the person whose name is on top of the list sometimes does not get an appointment when some of the persons lower on the list do. If the appointing officer chooses the second or third eligible, the No. 1 eligible does not get a job at once, but stays on the list until he is appointed or the list is terminated.

X. HOW TO PASS THE INTERVIEW TEST

The examination for which you applied requires an oral interview test. You have already taken the written test and you are now being called for the interview test – the final part of the formal examination.

You may think that it is not possible to prepare for an interview test and that there are no procedures to follow during an interview. Our purpose is to point out some things you can do in advance that will help you and some good rules to follow and pitfalls to avoid while you are being interviewed.

What is an interview supposed to test?

The written examination is designed to test the technical knowledge and competence of the candidate; the oral is designed to evaluate intangible qualities, not readily measured otherwise, and to establish a list showing the relative fitness of each candidate – as measured against his competitors – for the position sought. Scoring is not on the basis of "right" and "wrong," but on a sliding scale of values ranging from "not passable" to "outstanding." As a matter of fact, it is possible to achieve a relatively low score without a single "incorrect" answer because of evident weakness in the qualities being measured.

Occasionally, an examination may consist entirely of an oral test – either an individual or a group oral. In such cases, information is sought concerning the technical knowledges and abilities of the candidate, since there has been no written examination for this purpose. More commonly, however, an oral test is used to supplement a written examination.

Who conducts interviews?

The composition of oral boards varies among different jurisdictions. In nearly all, a representative of the personnel department serves as chairman. One of the members of the board may be a representative of the department in which the candidate would work. In some cases, "outside experts" are used, and, frequently, a businessman or some other representative of the general public is asked to serve. Labor and management or other special groups may be represented. The aim is to secure the services of experts in the appropriate field.

However the board is composed, it is a good idea (and not at all improper or unethical) to ascertain in advance of the interview who the members are and what groups they represent. When you are introduced to them, you will have some idea of their backgrounds and interests, and at least you will not stutter and stammer over their names.

What should be done before the interview?

While knowledge about the board members is useful and takes some of the surprise element out of the interview, there is other preparation which is more substantive. It *is* possible to prepare for an oral interview – in several ways:

1) Keep a copy of your application and review it carefully before the interview

This may be the only document before the oral board, and the starting point of the interview. Know what education and experience you have listed there, and the sequence and dates of all of it. Sometimes the board will ask you to review the highlights of your experience for them; you should not have to hem and haw doing it.

2) Study the class specification and the examination announcement

Usually, the oral board has one or both of these to guide them. The qualities, characteristics or knowledges required by the position sought are stated in these documents. They offer valuable clues as to the nature of the oral interview. For example, if the job involves supervisory responsibilities, the announcement will usually indicate that knowledge of modern supervisory methods and the qualifications of the candidate as a supervisor will be tested. If so, you can expect such questions, frequently in the form of a hypothetical situation which you are expected to solve. NEVER go into an oral without knowledge of the duties and responsibilities of the job you seek.

3) Think through each qualification required

Try to visualize the kind of questions you would ask if you were a board member. How well could you answer them? Try especially to appraise your own knowledge and background in each area, *measured against the job sought*, and identify any areas in which you are weak. Be critical and realistic – do not flatter yourself.

4) Do some general reading in areas in which you feel you may be weak

For example, if the job involves supervision and your past experience has NOT, some general reading in supervisory methods and practices, particularly in the field of human relations, might be useful. Do NOT study agency procedures or detailed manuals. The oral board will be testing your understanding and capacity, not your memory.

5) Get a good night's sleep and watch your general health and mental attitude

You will want a clear head at the interview. Take care of a cold or any other minor ailment, and of course, no hangovers.

What should be done on the day of the interview?

Now comes the day of the interview itself. Give yourself plenty of time to get there. Plan to arrive somewhat ahead of the scheduled time, particularly if your appointment is in the fore part of the day. If a previous candidate fails to appear, the board might be ready for you a bit early. By early afternoon an oral board is almost invariably behind schedule if there are many candidates, and you may have to wait. Take along a book or magazine to read, or your application to review, but leave any extraneous material in the waiting room when you go in for your interview. In any event, relax and compose yourself.

The matter of dress is important. The board is forming impressions about you – from your experience, your manners, your attitude, and your appearance. Give your personal appearance careful attention. Dress your best, but not your flashiest. Choose conservative, appropriate clothing, and be sure it is immaculate. This is a business interview, and your appearance should indicate that you regard it as such. Besides, being well groomed and properly dressed will help boost your confidence.

Sooner or later, someone will call your name and escort you into the interview room. *This is it.* From here on you are on your own. It is too late for any more preparation. But remember, you asked for this opportunity to prove your fitness, and you are here because your request was granted.

What happens when you go in?

The usual sequence of events will be as follows: The clerk (who is often the board stenographer) will introduce you to the chairman of the oral board, who will introduce you to the other members of the board. Acknowledge the introductions before you sit down. Do not be surprised if you find a microphone facing you or a stenotypist sitting by. Oral interviews are usually recorded in the event of an appeal or other review.

Usually the chairman of the board will open the interview by reviewing the highlights of your education and work experience from your application – primarily for the benefit of the other members of the board, as well as to get the material into the record. Do not interrupt or comment unless there is an error or significant misinterpretation; if that is the case, do not hesitate. But do not quibble about insignificant matters. Also, he will usually ask you some question about your education, experience or your present job – partly to get you to start talking and to establish the interviewing "rapport." He may start the actual questioning, or turn it over to one of the other members. Frequently, each member undertakes the questioning on a particular area, one in which he is perhaps most competent, so you can expect each member to participate in the examination. Because time is limited, you may also expect some rather abrupt switches in the direction the questioning takes, so do not be upset by it. Normally, a board member will not pursue a single line of questioning unless he discovers a particular strength or weakness.

After each member has participated, the chairman will usually ask whether any member has any further questions, then will ask you if you have anything you wish to add. Unless you are expecting this question, it may floor you. Worse, it may start you off on an extended, extemporaneous speech. The board is not usually seeking more information. The question is principally to offer you a last opportunity to present further qualifications or to indicate that you have nothing to add. So, if you feel that a significant qualification or characteristic has been overlooked, it is proper to point it out in a sentence or so. Do not compliment the board on the thoroughness of their examination – they have been sketchy, and you know it. If you wish, merely say, "No thank you, I have nothing further to add." This is a point where you can "talk yourself out" of a good impression or fail to present an important bit of information. Remember, *you close the interview yourself.*

The chairman will then say, "That is all, Mr. _____, thank you." Do not be startled; the interview is over, and quicker than you think. Thank him, gather your belongings and take your leave. Save your sigh of relief for the other side of the door.

How to put your best foot forward

Throughout this entire process, you may feel that the board individually and collectively is trying to pierce your defenses, seek out your hidden weaknesses and embarrass and confuse you. Actually, this is not true. They are obliged to make an appraisal of your qualifications for the job you are seeking, and they want to see you in your best light. Remember, they must interview all candidates and a non-cooperative candidate may become a failure in spite of their best efforts to bring out his qualifications. Here are 15 suggestions that will help you:

1) Be natural – Keep your attitude confident, not cocky

If you are not confident that you can do the job, do not expect the board to be. Do not apologize for your weaknesses, try to bring out your strong points. The board is interested in a positive, not negative, presentation. Cockiness will antagonize any board member and make him wonder if you are covering up a weakness by a false show of strength.

2) Get comfortable, but don't lounge or sprawl

Sit erectly but not stiffly. A careless posture may lead the board to conclude that you are careless in other things, or at least that you are not impressed by the importance of the occasion. Either conclusion is natural, even if incorrect. Do not fuss with your clothing, a pencil or an ashtray. Your hands may occasionally be useful to emphasize a point; do not let them become a point of distraction.

3) Do not wisecrack or make small talk

This is a serious situation, and your attitude should show that you consider it as such. Further, the time of the board is limited – they do not want to waste it, and neither should you.

4) Do not exaggerate your experience or abilities

In the first place, from information in the application or other interviews and sources, the board may know more about you than you think. Secondly, you probably will not get away with it. An experienced board is rather adept at spotting such a situation, so do not take the chance.

5) If you know a board member, do not make a point of it, yet do not hide it

Certainly you are not fooling him, and probably not the other members of the board. Do not try to take advantage of your acquaintanceship – it will probably do you little good.

6) Do not dominate the interview

Let the board do that. They will give you the clues – do not assume that you have to do all the talking. Realize that the board has a number of questions to ask you, and do not try to take up all the interview time by showing off your extensive knowledge of the answer to the first one.

7) Be attentive

You only have 20 minutes or so, and you should keep your attention at its sharpest throughout. When a member is addressing a problem or question to you, give him your undivided attention. Address your reply principally to him, but do not exclude the other board members.

8) Do not interrupt

A board member may be stating a problem for you to analyze. He will ask you a question when the time comes. Let him state the problem, and wait for the question.

9) Make sure you understand the question

Do not try to answer until you are sure what the question is. If it is not clear, restate it in your own words or ask the board member to clarify it for you. However, do not haggle about minor elements.

10) Reply promptly but not hastily

A common entry on oral board rating sheets is "candidate responded readily," or "candidate hesitated in replies." Respond as promptly and quickly as you can, but do not jump to a hasty, ill-considered answer.

11) Do not be peremptory in your answers

A brief answer is proper – but do not fire your answer back. That is a losing game from your point of view. The board member can probably ask questions much faster than you can answer them.

12) Do not try to create the answer you think the board member wants

He is interested in what kind of mind you have and how it works – not in playing games. Furthermore, he can usually spot this practice and will actually grade you down on it.

13) Do not switch sides in your reply merely to agree with a board member

Frequently, a member will take a contrary position merely to draw you out and to see if you are willing and able to defend your point of view. Do not start a debate, yet do not surrender a good position. If a position is worth taking, it is worth defending.

14) Do not be afraid to admit an error in judgment if you are shown to be wrong
The board knows that you are forced to reply without any opportunity for careful consideration. Your answer may be demonstrably wrong. If so, admit it and get on with the interview.

15) Do not dwell at length on your present job
The opening question may relate to your present assignment. Answer the question but do not go into an extended discussion. You are being examined for a *new* job, not your present one. As a matter of fact, try to phrase ALL your answers in terms of the job for which you are being examined.

Basis of Rating
Probably you will forget most of these "do's" and "don'ts" when you walk into the oral interview room. Even remembering them all will not ensure you a passing grade. Perhaps you did not have the qualifications in the first place. But remembering them will help you to put your best foot forward, without treading on the toes of the board members.

Rumor and popular opinion to the contrary notwithstanding, an oral board wants you to make the best appearance possible. They know you are under pressure – but they also want to see how you respond to it as a guide to what your reaction would be under the pressures of the job you seek. They will be influenced by the degree of poise you display, the personal traits you show and the manner in which you respond.

ABOUT THIS BOOK

This book contains tests divided into Examination Sections. Go through each test, answering every question in the margin. We have also attached a sample answer sheet at the back of the book that can be removed and used. At the end of each test look at the answer key and check your answers. On the ones you got wrong, look at the right answer choice and learn. Do not fill in the answers first. Do not memorize the questions and answers, but understand the answer and principles involved. On your test, the questions will likely be different from the samples. Questions are changed and new ones added. If you understand these past questions you should have success with any changes that arise. Tests may consist of several types of questions. We have additional books on each subject should more study be advisable or necessary for you. Finally, the more you study, the better prepared you will be. This book is intended to be the last thing you study before you walk into the examination room. Prior study of relevant texts is also recommended. NLC publishes some of these in our Fundamental Series. Knowledge and good sense are important factors in passing your exam. Good luck also helps. So now study this Passbook, absorb the material contained within and take that knowledge into the examination. Then do your best to pass that exam.

EXAMINATION SECTION

EXAMINATION SECTION
TEST 1

DIRECTIONS: Each question or incomplete statement is followed by several suggested answers or completions. Select the one that BEST answers the question or completes the statement. *PRINT THE LETTER OF THE CORRECT ANSWER IN THE SPACE AT THE RIGHT.*

1. The human thyroid requires

    A. potassium
    B. carbohydrate
    C. iodine
    D. sulphur

    1._____

2. The passage of dissolved food from the cavity of the alimentary canal into the bloodstream is known as

    A. assimilation
    B. anabolism
    C. catabolism
    D. osmosis

    2._____

3. The enzyme which functions ONLY in an acid medium is

    A. amylopsin   B. pepsin   C. ptyalin   D. trypsin

    3._____

4. The change of nutrients into protoplasm is called

    A. anabolism
    B. catabolism
    C. karyokinesis
    D. osmosis

    4._____

5. Fat is digested MAINLY in the

    A. gall bladder
    B. large intestine
    C. mouth
    D. small intestine

    5._____

6. The passage of digested substances into the villi for distribution through the body is called

    A. absorption
    B. metabolism
    C. anabolism
    D. peristalsis

    6._____

7. Bile salts are valuable as digestive agents for fats because they

    A. supply the proper chemical medium
    B. emulsify
    C. neutralize
    D. increase surface tension

    7._____

8. Flavinoids which are effective in human health are

    A. biotics
    B. bioflavinoids
    C. neoflavinoids
    D. vitamins

    8._____

9. Salts which affect the alkalinity or acidity of protoplasm have

    A. osmotic action
    B. buffer action
    C. reduction
    D. condensation

    9._____

1

10. The mineral which maintains osmotic pressure is

   A. potassium   B. sodium   C. magnesium   D. iron

11. The process of hydrogenation converts

   A. salt water to fresh water
   B. unsaturated fats to saturated fats
   C. fatty acids to cholesterol
   D. cholesterol to fatty acids

12. Amino acids are absorbed MAINLY in the

   A. intestine   B. stomach   C. pancreas   D. liver

13. Uric acid results from

   A. vitamin deficiency
   B. metabolism of purines
   C. digestion of carbohydrates
   D. injection of nicotine

14. An enzyme that produces digestion products which do not set to form a gel is

   A. protease   B. bromelin   C. diastase   D. lycine

15. As a result of the metabolic processes, the body

   A. can form protein from fat
   B. cannot form carbohydrate from protein
   C. cannot form fat from protein
   D. can form carbohydrate from protein

16. Which of the following minerals is found in GREATEST abundance in the human body?

   A. Phosphorus
   B. Calcium
   C. Iron
   D. Iodine

17. The enzyme of the gastric juice which aids in the digestion of milk is

   A. trypsin   B. amylopsin   C. rennin   D. ptyalin

18. The digestive enzyme which functions in an acid medium is

   A. pepsin   B. ptyalin   C. trypsin   D. amylopsin

19. Ascorbic acid is less susceptible to oxidation processes when it is

   A. alone
   B. combined with an alkali
   C. combined with an acid
   D. thoroughly aerated

20. In weight control, the MOST important reason of the following, for slow increase or decrease of weight is to make sure that the person

   A. is not forced to accept radical changes
   B. changes his eating pattern
   C. is allowed to adjust gradually
   D. avoids digestive upsets

21. During digestion, proteins are reduced to

    A. ascorbic acid
    B. amino acids
    C. glucose
    D. glycogen

22. When water is the chemical that causes changes in nutrients during digestion, the procedure is referred to as

    A. hydrocarbons
    B. carbonizing
    C. hydrolysis
    D. hydroponics

23. Of the following, the nutrient that does NOT act as a regulator of body processes is

    A. a vitamin   B. fat   C. water   D. a mineral

24. The glands involved in the digestion of starches are the

    A. spleen   B. salivary   C. thyroid   D. adrenal

25. Retarded digestion of cooked protein is caused by

    A. chemical change in the food
    B. physical change in the food
    C. destruction of bacteria
    D. slow cooking in moist heat

26. An important function of protein is to regulate

    A. body temperature
    B. glandular secretions
    C. specific dynamic action of foodstuffs
    D. the buffer action in the bloodstream

27. The normal source of insulin in the human body is the

    A. liver
    B. thymus
    C. pancreas
    D. pineal gland

28. The pathway of excretion of the nitrogenous end products of protein metabolism is the

    A. lungs
    B. skin
    C. kidneys
    D. large intestine

29. Carbohydrate stored in the liver is

    A. galleass
    B. glycogen
    C. liepstarch
    D. galactose

30. Carbohydrates are especially good for

    A. energy and endurance
    B. building bones
    C. weight gain
    D. Vitamin C

KEY (CORRECT ANSWERS)

1.	C	16.	B
2.	D	17.	C
3.	B	18.	A
4.	B	19.	C
5.	D	20.	B
6.	A	21.	B
7.	B	22.	C
8.	B	23.	B
9.	B	24.	B
10.	B	25.	A
11.	B	26.	D
12.	A	27.	C
13.	B	28.	C
14.	C	29.	B
15.	D	30.	A

TEST 2

DIRECTIONS: Each question or incomplete statement is followed by several suggested answers or completions. Select the one that BEST answers the question or completes the statement. *PRINT THE LETTER OF THE CORRECT ANSWER IN THE SPACE AT THE RIGHT.*

1. The digestive secretion that is acid in reaction is   1.____

    A. saliva
    B. gastric juice
    C. pancreatic juice
    D. bile

2. Enzymes   2.____

    A. cause food changes
    B. are activated by boiling
    C. dissolve osmotic membranes
    D. increase reaction at freezing point

3. An intermediate product in the digestion of starch is   3.____

    A. dextrin   B. cerine   C. maltine   D. fibrinogen

4. Amino acids are substances containing   4.____

    A. hydrogen   B. nitrogen   C. oxygen   D. carbon

5. Digestive secretions of the human body contain chemical compounds called   5.____

    A. peptones
    B. polysaccharides
    C. proteoses
    D. enzymes

6. Amino acids are absorbed through the   6.____

    A. stomach
    B. liver
    C. intestines
    D. pancreas

7. The clotting of blood is aided by   7.____

    A. phosphorus
    B. calcium
    C. iron
    D. copper

8. The mineral that is responsible for the alkaline reaction of the human blood is   8.____

    A. calcium
    B. phosphorus
    C. iodine
    D. iron

9. Digestion of food is helped by having your mealtimes   9.____

    A. hurried   B. happy   C. worried   D. exciting

10. The alternate contractions and relaxations which constitute the normal beating of the heart are dependent in part upon the presence of _____ salts.   10.____

    A. calcium
    B. calcium and sodium
    C. potassium and sodium
    D. calcium, sodium, and potassium

11. A catalytic agent that brings about the normal metabolism of carbohydrates in all cells of the body is

    A. insulin
    B. riboflavin
    C. glucose
    D. thiamin

12. Vitamin A helps to

    A. give energy
    B. stimulate an appetite
    C. prevent eye and nose infection
    D. aid digestion

13. The body uses calcium for making

    A. scar tissue
    B. fat
    C. bone
    D. fingernails

14. A partially complete protein is one which

    A. is capable of maintaining growth but not life
    B. contains all the essential amino acids except glycinine
    C. is capable of maintaining neither life nor growth
    D. is capable of maintaining life but not growth

15. Salts affecting acidity or alkalinity of protoplasm have the effect of

    A. osmotic action
    B. condensation
    C. reduction
    D. buffer action

16. An acid ash is yielded by body oxidation of

    A. meats
    B. citrus fruits
    C. potatoes
    D. cream

17. The presence of acetone in urine indicates faulty metabolism of

    A. proteins
    B. carbohydrates
    C. fats
    D. minerals

18. A vitamin preparation given merely to satisfy a patient is being used as a

    A. dilative
    B. pacific
    C. placebo
    D. tranquilizer

19. The organ, the secretion of which neutralizes some poisons and dissolves cholesterol is the

    A. spleen   B. thyroid   C. pancreas   D. liver

20. The PRINCIPAL element which maintains osmotic pressure in the human system is

    A. iron   B. potassium   C. magnesium   D. sodium

21. The nutritive value of a protein is ultimately dependent upon its 21.____

    A. digestibility
    B. meat source
    C. connective tissue content
    D. amino acid content

22. In fever conditions, the basal metabolism of a person as compared to the norm is 22.____

    A. lower B. higher C. constant D. unchanged

23. Digested food is absorbed MAINLY in the 23.____

    A. small intestine   B. stomach
    C. large intestine   D. esophagus

24. The digestion of protein is accomplished by the action of the enzymes 24.____

    A. pepsin, trypsin, erepsin
    B. glycerol, lipase, amylopsis
    C. lecithin, cystine, lysine
    D. glycogen, ptyalin, galactose

25. In comparison with proteins, fats contain LESS 25.____

    A. carbon   B. hydrogen
    C. phosphorus   D. nitrogen

26. The gland which produces insulin is the 26.____

    A. spleen B. pituitary C. thymus D. pancreas

27. The process of hydrogenation converts 27.____

    A. salt water to fresh water
    B. unsaturated fats to saturated fats
    C. fatty acids to cholesterol
    D. cholesterol to fatty acids

28. In the digestion of starch, an intermediate product is 28.____

    A. dextrin   B. fibrinogen
    C. cerine   D. maltine

29. Amino acids are absorbed MAINLY in the 29.____

    A. stomach B. liver C. pancreas D. intestine

30. In anabolism, the number of calories yielded by one gram of hydrocarbon is 30.____

    A. six B. seven C. eight D. nine

KEY (CORRECT ANSWERS)

1.	B	16.	A
2.	A	17.	C
3.	A	18.	C
4.	B	19.	D
5.	D	20.	D
6.	C	21.	D
7.	B	22.	B
8.	B	23.	A
9.	B	24.	A
10.	B	25.	D
11.	A	26.	D
12.	C	27.	B
13.	C	28.	A
14.	B	29.	D
15.	D	30.	D

EXAMINATION SECTION
TEST 1

DIRECTIONS: Each question or incomplete statement is followed by several suggested answers or completions. Select the one that BEST answers the question or completes the statement. *PRINT THE LETTER OF THE CORRECT ANSWER IN THE SPACE AT THE RIGHT.*

1. In substituting non-fat dried milk for whole milk in a reducing diet, it is important to consider that the dried milk has a lowered content of calories and also a lowered content of

   A. vitamin A
   B. calcium
   C. thiamin
   D. ascorbic acid

   1.____

2. The PRIMARY role of legumes in our menus is that of providing

   A. economy and variety
   B. protein and vitamins
   C. flavor and color
   D. carbohydrate and protein

   2.____

3. One pound of body fat is equivalent to APPROXIMATELY _____ calories.

   A. 1000   B. 2000   C. 4000   D. 3000

   3.____

4. The vitamins present in meat are, in general, limited to

   A. B-complex
   B. vitamin A
   C. ascorbic acid
   D. ergosterol

   4.____

5. The nutrients MOST commonly lacking in American diets are

   A. ascorbic acid and riboflavin
   B. calcium and vitamin C
   C. protein and carbohydrates
   D. vitamin A and thiamine

   5.____

6. Glucose and fructose are examples of

   A. disaccharides
   B. polysaccharides
   C. saccharines
   D. monosaccharides

   6.____

7. Of the following, the food containing a complete protein is

   A. navy beans
   B. almonds
   C. beef round
   D. gelatin

   7.____

8. The MOST important of the nutritive contributions made by cereals in the diet is their content of

   A. B-complex vitamins
   B. minerals
   C. protein
   D. carbohydrate

   8.____

9. Loss of vitamin C content during cooking is increased by

   A. excessive stirring
   B. low cooking temperature
   C. low storage temperature
   D. use of a cover on the cooking utensil

   9.____

10. A research project to improve the world-wide protein deficiency was sponsored recently by

    A. UNICEF
    B. ICNND
    C. India
    D. U.S. Department of Agriculture

11. An individual with coronary heart disease should

    A. keep the fat intake low
    B. have a high cholesterol intake
    C. eat only hydrogenated fats
    D. have a medium to high sodium intake

12. Vitamin A is

    A. water-soluble
    B. a precursor of carotene
    C. useful in preventing rickets
    D. fat-soluble

13. The vitamin A value of carrots is HIGHEST when the carrots are

    A. harvested young as baby carrots
    B. grown in rich loam
    C. mature, of at least 2" crown diameter
    D. cooked in boiling salted water

14. Loss of nutrients in frozen vegetables frequently occurs when they are

    A. frozen whole   B. dehydro frozen
    C. blanched   D. sliced or chopped

15. Which of the following foods contains the calcium equivalent to that in one glass of milk?

    A. One-third cup evaporated milk
    B. Three ounces American cheese
    C. One-half cup turnip greens
    D. One dozen soft shelled clams

16. Which of the following vitamins is NOT water soluble?

    A. Vitamin C   B. Thiamin
    C. Niacin   D. Vitamin D

17. It is recommended that milk not be subjected to direct rays of the sun because it might destroy one of the following nutrients:

    A. Thiamin   B. Niacin
    C. Riboflavin   D. Pyridoxin

18. A two-ounce portion of freshly opened canned juice which will contain the largest amount of ascorbic acid is

    A. lemon   B. grapefruit
    C. tomato   D. orange

19. Baking soda should not be used in vegetable cookery because it
    A. gives a bitter flavor
    B. destroys the chlorophyll
    C. destroys thiamin
    D. destroys vitamin A

20. The toasting of a piece of bread is an example of
    A. gelatinization   B. mastication
    C. carbonation   D. dextrinization

21. A rich source of vitamin K is
    A. butter   B. spinach   C. oranges   D. milk

22. The nutrient losses in the dehydration process are similar to those in
    A. sterilization   B. electronic cooking
    C. evaporation   D. pasteurization

23. A safe daily dietary for a reduction regimen will supply APPROXIMATELY _____ calories.
    A. 2500   B. 1500   C. 2000   D. 3000

24. When a diabetic needing insulin eats more food than his prescribed diet allows, a possible resulting danger is the development of
    A. shock   B. stroke   C. acidosis   D. hemorrhage

25. A good source of riboflavin is
    A. milk   B. onions
    C. vegetable fats   D. orange juice

KEY (CORRECT ANSWERS)

1. A
2. A
3. C
4. A
5. B

6. D
7. C
8. A
9. A
10. A

11. A
12. D
13. C
14. D
15. A

16. D
17. C
18. C
19. D
20. D

21. B
22. D
23. B
24. C
25. A

TEST 2

DIRECTIONS: Each question or incomplete statement is followed by several suggested answers or completions. Select the one that BEST answers the question or completes the statement. *PRINT THE LETTER OF THE CORRECT ANSWER IN THE SPACE AT THE RIGHT.*

1. Of the following 100 gram portions of fresh substance, the one which yields the MOST iron is 1.____

    A. beef, all lean
    B. egg yolk
    C. dried beans
    D. dried peas

2. The following foods tend to diminish acidity in the urine: 2.____

    A. Tomatoes, oranges, apricots, pineapple
    B. Tomatoes, cranberries, plums, apricots
    C. Tomatoes, prunes, apricots, pineapple
    D. Cranberries, oranges, apricots, pineapple

3. The vitamin MOST readily destroyed in cooking is 3.____

    A. vitamin A
    B. ascorbic acid
    C. vitamin D
    D. riboflavin

4. The amount of calcium required for a one-year-old child is 4.____

    A. less than is needed by a very active man
    B. as much as is needed by a pregnant woman
    C. more than that needed by a very active woman
    D. more than that needed by a ten-year-old child

5. The bodily requirement of protein needed by a man on a reducing diet is 5.____

    A. less than the amount needed on his normal diet
    B. more than the amount needed on his normal diet
    C. the same amount that is required by an adolescent boy
    D. the same amount that is required on his normal diet

6. When food is taken into the stomach, 6.____

    A. protein food stays longer than carbohydrate
    B. emulsified fats leave first
    C. mixtures of fat and protein are quickly digested
    D. fat leaves before protein

7. Injections of insulin may be needed 7.____

    A. to promote oxidation
    B. to raise the concentration of glucose in the blood
    C. to lower the concentration of glucose in the blood
    D. replace adrenaline

8. *Depot fat* refers to 8.____

13

A. deposits of body fat as reserve fuel
B. fat the body cannot synthesize
C. fat the body cannot re-form
D. fatty acids and glycerols which cannot be re-synthesized by the body

9. An example of a fatty acid is _____ acid.

   A. ascorbic   B. lactic   C. lauric   D. acetic

10. Although milk is said to be the perfect food, it is particularly deficient in one of the following:

    A. Iron   B. Vitamin C
    C. Vitamin D   D. Sulfur

11. The number of calories yielded by the anabolism of one gram of carbohydrates is

    A. two   B. four   C. six   D. ten

12. Egg yolk is rich in

    A. manganese   B. calcium   C. phosphorus   D. potassium

13. For normal nutrition, the tissues of the body must be in a state of saturation with respect to vitamin

    A. A   B. B   C. C   D. E

14. In nutrition, the utilization of the absorbed products is called

    A. anabolism   B. osmosis
    C. metabolism   D. catabolism

15. The food which will produce an acid ash is

    A. dried beans   B. carrots
    C. rice   D. sweet potatoes

16. Carbohydrates are classified chemically according to the number of

    A. oxides   B. saccharides
    C. hydroxides   D. carbides

17. The MAXIMUM number of hours during which extracted exposed orange juice will retain effective vitamin C content is

    A. 12   B. 24   C. 36   D. 48

18. Irradiation of foods produces vitamin

    A. A   B. B   C. C   D. D

19. Eggs supplement milk because they provide

    A. protein   B. fat   C. iron   D. vitamins

20. The eating of coarse foods helps in

    A. digesting starches   B. digesting proteins
    C. preventing constipation   D. repairing muscles

21. Water is a
   A. regulator of body processes
   B. vitamin-rich food
   C. destroyer of vitamins
   D. fuel food

22. The energy value of the foodstuffs that oxidize in the body can be measured by
   A. calories
   B. body weight
   C. weight of food
   D. quality of the food

23. A good breakfast judged according to growth elements contained in the food would be
   A. orange juice, toast, and coffee
   B. bacon, waffles, and syrup
   C. cereal, milk, rolls, and butter
   D. prunes, cereal, toast, and milk

24. A food that is rich in mineral matter is
   A. white flour
   B. cabbage
   C. butter
   D. ready-to-eat cereals

25. Nutritionally, the BEST way to serve fruits is to
   A. bake them
   B. serve them raw
   C. steam them
   D. stew them

KEY (CORRECT ANSWERS)

1. A		11. B	
2. A		12. C	
3. A		13. C	
4. B		14. C	
5. B		15. C	
6. C		16. B	
7. C		17. B	
8. A		18. D	
9. C		19. C	
10. A		20. C	

21. A
22. A
23. D
24. D
25. B

TEST 3

DIRECTIONS: Each question or incomplete statement is followed by several suggested answers or completions. Select the one that BEST answers the question or completes the statement. *PRINT THE LETTER OF THE CORRECT ANSWER IN THE SPACE AT THE RIGHT.*

1. A rich source of riboflavin is 1.____
   A. turnips
   B. legumes
   C. whole grains
   D. milk and its products

2. To promote normal vision is a function of vitamin 2.____
   A. A   B. B   C. C   D. D

3. To stimulate the appetite is the function of vitamin 3.____
   A. A   B. B_1 C. C   D. D

4. Proteins are classified according to the contained amount of 4.____
   A. oxygen
   B. carbon
   C. amino acids
   D. purins

5. Rickets is a deficiency disease due to an insufficient supply of vitamin 5.____
   A. A   B. B   C. C   D. D

6. Nicotinic acid is used in the treatment of 6.____
   A. psoriasis   B. pellagra   C. beri-beri   D. scurvy

7. Cane sugar is 7.____
   A. invertase   B. sucrose   C. dextrose   D. levulose

8. Surplus vitamin A is stored in the 8.____
   A. kidneys   B. liver   C. blood   D. muscles

9. Fish liver oils are the richest source of vitamin 9.____
   A. A   B. B   C. C   D. D

10. Direct irradiation increases the content of vitamin 10.____
    A. A   B. B   C. C   D. D

11. The number of calories yielded by the anabolism of one gram of fat is 11.____
    A. 6   B. 7   C. 8   D. 9

12. The LEAST expensive simple sugar is 12.____
    A. levulose   B. lactose   C. glucose   D. galactose

13. The element that constitutes the major portion of the weight of the human body is 13.____
    A. copper   B. sodium   C. calcium   D. iron

14. The development of the disease known as beri-beri is due to a marked deficiency of vitamin   14.____

    A. A   B. B   C. B_1 D. C

15. Compared with whole cereals, soybeans have   15.____

    A. equal vitamin A values   B. greater cellulose content
    C. lesser vitamin A values   D. greater vitamin A values

16. A complete protein found in milk is   16.____

    A. gliadin   B. ovalbumin   C. casein   D. albumin

17. Resistance to infection is a function of vitamin   17.____

    A. A   B. B   C. C   D. D

18. A fat-soluble vitamin is   18.____

    A. A
    C. C
    B. B_1
    D. riboflavin

19. The largest percentage of gluten protein is found in   19.____

    A. oats   B. barley   C. rye   D. wheat

20. The body can produce vitamin   20.____

    A. A   B. B   C. C   D. D

21. The food that will produce an alkaline ash is   21.____

    A. oatmeal   B. eggs   C. oysters   D. bananas

22. Compared with the average reported by the Department of Agriculture for whole grain wheat flour, enriched flour contains iron and thiamine _____ average.   22.____

    A. exactly at the   B. above the
    C. approximately at   D. below the

23. The nutrients that can be purchased in the fall at lowest cost per pound of such nutrients is   23.____

    A. kidney beans   B. oranges
    C. chopped beef   D. flounder

24. The RICHEST food source of vitamin A is   24.____

    A. milk   B. egg yolk
    C. spinach   D. carrots

25. Efficient utilization of both calcium and phosphorus depends on a supply of vitamins   25.____

    A. A, B, E   B. B, D, G   C. A, C, D   D. C, E, G

KEY (CORRECT ANSWERS)

1.	D	11.	D
2.	A	12.	C
3.	B	13.	C
4.	C	14.	B
5.	D	15.	D
6.	B	16.	C
7.	B	17.	A
8.	B	18.	A
9.	D	19.	D
10.	D	20.	D

21. D
22. C
23. A
24. C
25. C

———

TEST 4

DIRECTIONS: Each question or incomplete statement is followed by several suggested answers or completions. Select the one that BEST answers the question or completes the statement. *PRINT THE LETTER OF THE CORRECT ANSWER IN THE SPACE AT THE RIGHT.*

1. The part of broccoli which is RICHEST in important nutritive content is the   1._____
   A. stem   B. leaf   C. flowerlet   D. root

2. Vitamin loss in cooking frozen non-acid vegetables is MOST commonly due to   2._____
   A. rapid boiling   B. overcooking
   C. leaching   D. oxidation

3. Of the following, the only substance which affects the nutritive value of bread is   3._____
   A. yeast   B. bread softener
   C. mold inhibitor   D. bran

4. The group which contains a foodstuff NOT soluble in water is   4._____
   A. calcium, iron, thiamine, niacin
   B. vitamins B, G, niacin, and C
   C. vitamins A, D, niacin, and E
   D. phosphorus, iron, calcium, iodine

5. *Enriched* flours and breads are wheat products to which have been added specific amounts of thiamin, niacin, and   5._____
   A. iron   B. riboflavin and iron
   C. calcium and iron   D. ascorbic acid and iron

6. A diet of commonly available foodstuffs will furnish a healthy person more than adequate amounts of all the known essential vitamins EXCEPT vitamin   6._____
   A. A   B. B   C. C   D. D

7. Which of the following should NOT be consumed by someone suffering from hypertension due to its naturally high salt content?   7._____
   A. Celery   B. Carrots   C. Rice   D. Bananas

8. A vegetable source of protein food is   8._____
   A. legumes   B. chutney
   C. gelatin   D. Irish moss

9. Of the following, a rich source of the vitamin B complex is   9._____
   A. seafoods   B. refined cereals
   C. citrus fruits   D. whole grains

10. The chemical name for vitamin C is _____ acid.   10._____
    A. cevitamic   B. citric   C. amino   D. lactic

19

11. Substances which promote growth and energy and help the body resist diseases are   11._____

    A. proteins B. amino acids
    C. fatty acids D. vitamins

12. A ketogenic diet is a diet with a high percentage of   12._____

    A. vitamins   B. fat   C. protein   D. minerals

13. Of the following, the LEAST costly, as well as the BEST source of calcium and phosphorus in a form in which it may be assimilated directly, is   13._____

    A. dried milk
    B. meat
    C. dried fruits and vegetables
    D. multiple-vitamin-mineral preparations

14. The diet of MOST Puerto Ricans is deficient in   14._____

    A. vitamin B and calcium
    B. carbohydrates, proteins, and cellulose
    C. protein, calcium, vitamin A, and riboflavin
    D. fats and carbohydrates

15. Cutting down the amount of cane sugar improves the average diet because sugar tends to   15._____

    A. cause diabetes
    B. stimulate the appetite
    C. cause overweight
    D. irritate the digestive tract

16. According to United States law, the percentage of milk fat by weight which butter MUST contain is not less than   16._____

    A. 75%   B. 80%   C. 65%   D. 90%

17. Iodine is necessary for the normal functioning of the   17._____

    A. red blood cells B. thyroid gland
    C. heart D. hemoglobin

18. The diet of a 72-year-old woman should include extra quantities of   18._____

    A. proteins B. vitamins
    C. minerals D. carbohydrates

19. Of the following foods, the one which could be included in a low residue diet is   19._____

    A. applesauce B. mashed potatoes
    C. steamed asparagus D. creamed celery

20. As an aid in making up the daily quota of calcium and phosphorus, serve   20._____

    A. soda crackers and fruit jelly
    B. pineapple juice to start the dinner
    C. milk puddings as desserts
    D. a peanut butter sandwich at lunch

21. Of the following foods, the RICHEST source of iodine is 21._____

    A. lake trout B. corn
    C. oranges   D. salmon

22. An element found in proteins but NOT found in carbohy-drates is 22._____

    A. nitrogen   B. carbon   C. oxygen   D. hydrogen

23. Foods such as custards, poached eggs, milk, toast, cereals, puddings, and ice cream are served when the prescribed diet is 23._____

    A. bland   B. liquids   C. soft   D. regular

24. Each of the vitamins below is correctly paired with the disease it helps to prevent EXCEPT vitamin 24._____

    A. A - pellagra   B. B_1 - beri-beri
    C. C - scurvy   D. D - rickets

25. Of the following, the BEST source of the vitamin which functions to condition the walls of blood vessels is 25._____

    A. carrots   B. milk
    C. orange juice   D. whole wheat bread

KEY (CORRECT ANSWERS)

1.	B	11.	D
2.	C	12.	B
3.	A	13.	A
4.	C	14.	C
5.	B	15.	C
6.	D	16.	B
7.	A	17.	B
8.	A	18.	B
9.	D	19.	B
10.	B	20.	C

21. D
22. A
23. C
24. A
25. C

TEST 5

DIRECTIONS: Each question or incomplete statement is followed by several suggested answers or completions. Select the one that BEST answers the question or completes the statement. *PRINT THE LETTER OF THE CORRECT ANSWER IN THE SPACE AT THE RIGHT.*

1. Body weight can be reduced at the rate of about one pound per week by the daily withdrawal from the bodily stores of about _____ calories.

    A. 500   B. 1000   C. 2000   D. 3000

2. The availability of iron derived from various sources depends on the

    A. form in which it occurs in the food
    B. supply of thiamin
    C. amount of iron-rich foods provided
    D. amount of iron required by the body

3. All of the following foods furnish approximately 100 calories EXCEPT

    A. 1 large orange
    B. 1 head lettuce
    C. 1 tbsp. butter
    D. 5/8 cup whole milk

4. Excess frost on a package of frozen vegetables indicates

    A. probable loss of vitamin C
    B. inferior packing
    C. inferior produce
    D. poor air circulation in the freezer

5. Caribbean children find it difficult to adjust to the usual foods of New York City because they are not accustomed to

    A. fresh fruits
    B. rice
    C. fresh eggs
    D. fresh milk

6. Dehydration of food by sunlight results in

    A. loss of vitamin C content
    B. increased bulk
    C. increased vitamin D
    D. lower calcium content

7. Of the following, the one which is MOST economical for protein re-enforcement of the diet is

    A. egg yolk
    B. ice cream
    C. cream cheese
    D. skim milk powder

8. The riboflavin content of a food is GREATLY lowered by exposure of the food to

    A. heat
    B. freezing temperature
    C. air
    D. sunlight

9. The chemical name for *animal starch* is 9.____

   A. glycogen B. glucose
   C. amylodextrin D. dextrose

10. According to the prevailing concept, a diet rich in unsaturated fatty acids can be labeled 10.____

    A. anti-atherogenic B. atherogenic
    C. anti-scorbutic D. nephritic

11. Compared with 16-20 year-old girls, 13-15 year-old girls need 11.____

    A. less iron B. less vitamin D
    C. more calcium D. more protein

12. To provide vitamin C, serve 12.____

    A. apricots B. whole wheat bread
    C. cole slaw D. cocoa

13. Compared with the recommended figure of 50%, the ACTUAL percentage of food calories derived from protective foods in the American diet is 13.____

    A. 20% B. 25% C. 33% D. 45%

14. To provide the basis for building red blood corpuscles, feed 14.____

    A. cream tapioca B. buttered toast
    C. yolk of egg D. white of egg

15. Salt water fish, as compared with fresh water fish, contain more 15.____

    A. iodine B. calcium C. copper D. magnesium

16. As an aid to make up the daily quota of calcium and phosphorus, serve 16.____

    A. water at mealtime
    B. milk puddings as desserts
    C. pineapple juice as an appetizer
    D. peanut butter on white bread

17. Potatoes are superior in nutritive value when 17.____

    A. cut in strips and fried
    B. cut up and boiled
    C. baked whole
    D. boiled whole without skins

18. An EXCELLENT source of fibrous material is 18.____

    A. pureed potato soup B. cream of wheat cereal
    C. mozzarella cheese D. escarole

19. For HIGHEST nutritive value at least cost, of the following choose 19.____

    A. meatloaf, soybeans, and vegetables
    B. round steak with brown rice
    C. meatballs and spaghetti
    D. braised mushrooms and liver steak

20. The extractives in meat are valuable because they

 A. provide energy
 B. are a source of iron
 C. supply vitamins
 D. aid digestion

21. Whole-grain cereals are preferred because they

 A. have flavor
 B. are easily prepared
 C. contain vitamins
 D. provide calories

22. The outside leaves of salad greens

 A. contain more vitamin A and iron
 B. make the salad crispy
 C. are more tender
 D. contain more roughage

23. The BEST dessert to provide additional protein in a meal is

 A. apple pie
 B. baked custard
 C. fruit jello
 D. apricot whip

24. Vitamin C is present in _____ milk.

 A. evaporated
 B. pasteurized
 C. raw
 D. condensed

25. The RICHEST vegetable source of riboflavin is

 A. lima beans
 B. fresh peas
 C. lettuce
 D. dried soybeans

KEY (CORRECT ANSWERS)

1.	A	11.	D
2.	A	12.	A
3.	B	13.	C
4.	A	14.	C
5.	D	15.	A
6.	A	16.	B
7.	D	17.	C
8.	D	18.	D
9.	A	19.	A
10.	A	20.	D

21. C
22. A
23. B
24. C
25. C

EXAMINATION SECTION
TEST 1

DIRECTIONS: Each question or incomplete statement is followed by several suggested answers or completions. Select the one that BEST answers the question or completes the statement. *PRINT THE LETTER OF THE CORRECT ANSWER IN THE SPACE AT THE RIGHT.*

1. In the last fifty years, the proportion of calories from milk, cheese, fruits, and vegetables in the American diet has

    A. remained the same B. doubled
    C. tripled D. quadrupled

    1.____

2. Interference with absorption of vitamin A may result from

    A. a diet heavy with bulk foods
    B. overconsumption of salad oils
    C. mineral oil in salad dressings
    D. low cholesterol diet

    2.____

3. Hypoglycemia is a condition of

    A. diseased eyes B. low blood sugar
    C. high blood sugar D. low purin content

    3.____

4. The term *trace elements* refers to

    A. minerals needed in very small amounts in nutrition
    B. substance which trace circulation in the body
    C. tools used in sewing
    D. potent drugs used as pain killer

    4.____

5. One of the EARLIEST symptoms of a thiamine deficiency is

    A. polyneuritis B. anorexia
    C. nyctalopia D. conjunctivitis

    5.____

6. In measuring vitamin A value in foods, the international unit is defined as the activity of

    A. 5.0 mg. calciferol B. 6.0 gm. tocopherol
    C. 6.0 gm. carotene D. 0.6 mcg. betacarotene

    6.____

7. The RICHEST food sources of folacin are

    A. livers and green leafy vegetables
    B. eggs and milk
    C. cereals
    D. fats

    7.____

8. Folacin is necessary for

    A. digestion of carbohydrates
    B. metabolism of sterols
    C. synthesis of chlorophyll
    D. hematopoiesis

    8.____

9. Avidin is a(n)
   A. vitamin B. protein C. fiber D. fabric

10. The liver is the storage depot in the body for vitamin
    A. A B. E C. C D. B

11. The anti-xerophthalmia vitamin is vitamin
    A. A B. B C. E D. K

12. Riboflavin is EASILY destroyed by
    A. alkalies and light
    B. acids and oxygen
    C. heat and agitation
    D. air and agitation

13. The material which destroys the activity of biotin is
    A. the protein found in uncooked egg white
    B. fluorides in drinking water
    C. iodides in medications
    D. fluorescent substances found in milk

14. The diet prescribed in diverticulitis is one that is
    A. high in calorie value
    B. high in roughage content
    C. low residue, bland
    D. high protein, bland

15. In typhoid fever, the diet should be
    A. *high* in calories and residue
    B. *low* in calories, high in residue
    C. *high* in calories, low in residue
    D. *high* in fruit juice content

16. Of the following, the HIGHEST in caloric value is one cupful
    A. strained honey
    B. orange juice
    C. sugar
    D. homogenized milk

17. Among the following, the BEST food source of thiamine is
    A. refined sugars
    B. fats
    C. egg white
    D. pork

18. In the list below, the BEST source of vitamin A is
    A. wheat germ
    B. pork
    C. milk
    D. spinach

19. A disadvantage resulting from the intake of mineral oil is that it
    A. adds calories
    B. reduces weight
    C. impairs the appetite
    D. dissolves vitamin A

20. The MAJOR influence in the decline of endemic goiter in the United States is the use of
    A. saffron oil
    B. homogenized milk
    C. iodized salt
    D. enriched cereals

21. Cretinism is a form of idiocy due to extreme deficiency of secretion by 21.____

    A. fat-soluble vitamins in the diet
    B. B-complex vitamins in the diet
    C. thyroid gland
    D. adrenal glands

22. Fuel value of foods is determined by use of a(n) 22.____

    A. caloric unit
    C. calciferol
    B. calorific unit
    D. calorimeter

23. For the average American, minerals of value as food supplements for the diet are calcium and 23.____

    A. phosphorus, sodium, and choline
    B. chlorine, magnesium, and iron
    C. phosphorus, iron, and iodine
    D. chlorine, iron, and manganese

24. For the average American, the vitamins of value as food supplements are thiamine, pyridoxine, riboflavin, calciferol, ascorbic acid, and 24.____

    A. niacin, B_{12}, A
    C. B_{12}, K, A
    B. B_6, B_{12}, folic acid
    D. B_{12}, A, E

25. Nyctalopia results from a lack of 25.____

    A. vitamin A
    C. citric acid
    B. fluorine
    D. flavinoids

KEY (CORRECT ANSWERS)

1.	B	11.	A
2.	C	12.	A
3.	B	13.	A
4.	A	14.	C
5.	B	15.	C
6.	D	16.	A
7.	A	17.	D
8.	D	18.	D
9.	B	19.	D
10.	A	20.	C

21. C
22. D
23. C
24. A
25. A

TEST 2

DIRECTIONS: Each question or incomplete statement is followed by several suggested answers or completions. Select the one that BEST answers the question or completes the statement. *PRINT THE LETTER OF THE CORRECT ANSWER IN THE SPACE AT THE RIGHT.*

1. The number of amino acids which are essential for human growth is 1.____

   A. 23 B. 8 C. 16 D. 6

2. Of the following statements, the one which expresses a food fallacy is: 2.____

   A. There are no *miracle* foods
   B. Canned foods can be left in their original containers without danger
   C. Vitamin tablets or concentrates are necessary for guarantee of an adequate diet
   D. Toasting a slice of bread will not alter its calorie content

3. The dietary contribution of fish is 3.____

   A. a high concentration of vitamin C
   B. a high concentration of vitamin B_{12}
   C. all the nutrients except carbohydrates
   D. a high concentration of iron

4. A component of vegetable oils and some fish which will increase exertion of bile salts and thus lower cholesterol is 4.____

   A. stearic acid   B. oleic acid
   C. linoleic acid   D. acrolein

5. The vitamin for which dried beans and peas are especially valuable is 5.____

   A. ascorbic acid   B. riboflavin
   C. niacin   D. thiamine

6. Especially notable for vitamin C content are the following: 6.____

   A. Dry beans and peas
   B. Raw cabbage and green peppers
   C. Crisp radishes and corn
   D. Okra and parsnips

7. A deficiency of riboflavin results in 7.____

   A. xerophthalmia   B. polyneuritis
   C. cutaneous lesions   D. chielosis

8. Of the following, the RICHEST source of vitamin E is 8.____

   A. liver   B. green leafy vegetables
   C. wheat germ oil   D. egg yolk

9. Of the following, the number of calories which MOST NEARLY approximates the daily fuel needs of a moderately active 25-year-old woman is 9.____

   A. 1500 B. 2000 C. 2500 D. 3500

10. Vitamin A food value is

    A. lacking in yams
    B. fairly constant in dairy products
    C. closely related to green coloring in vegetables
    D. closely related to sun available during growing time

11. The unit of measurement adopted for vitamins and minerals is based on the

    A. minimum daily requirement
    B. recommended dietary allowance
    C. available specific nutrients
    D. regional and cultural food patterns

12. Of the following, the RICHEST source of iron is

    A. citrus fruit   B. cheese
    C. apricots   D. whole wheat

13. The simplified method of calculating diabetic diets is based on

    A. the food exchange plan
    B. substituting orinase for insulin injections
    C. high vitamin content
    D. basic requirements of protein intake

14. When planning diets for diabetic patients, it is recommended that use be made, in proper amounts, of _____ foods.

    A. specialty   B. dietetically canned
    C. natural   D. fatty

15. Of the following fruits, the one which increases acidity in the body is

    A. tomatoes   B. oranges   C. prunes   D. peaches

16. Lipase

    A. controls the blood level of cholesterol
    B. is a polyunsaturated fatty acid
    C. is an enzyme
    D. gives color to green vegetables

17. Of the following, the foods which should be excluded from a minimum residue diet are

    A. milk and milk drinks   B. noodles and macaroni
    C. honey and jelly   D. carbonated beverages

18. Ascorbic acid is the chemical name for

    A. vitamin C   B. vitamin A
    C. a liver extract   D. an iron preparation

19. The real harm resulting from a ready and wide acceptance of food fads is that

    A. nutritional quackery costs several millions of dollars each year
    B. real dietitians and nutritionists lose prestige

C. proper medical attention for the patient is delayed
D. quacks and food faddists benefit

20. Of the following, the foods LOWEST in cholesterol are

    A. homogenized milk and light cream
    B. butter and cheese
    C. fruits and cereals
    D. fruits and cheese

21. Cheese is rich in

    A. calcium   B. potassium   C. iron   D. manganese

22. The anti-hemorrhagic vitamin is

    A. niacin   B. vitamin A
    C. vitamin K   D. riboflavin

23. A complete protein is found in

    A. navy beans   B. peas
    C. lean meat   D. gelatin

24. Butter provides vitamin

    A. G   B. B_1 C. D   D. C

25. The vitamin that is LESS easily destroyed in an acid medium than when the medium is alkaline is

    A. A   B. B   C. C   D. D

KEY (CORRECT ANSWERS)

1. B
2. C
3. C
4. C
5. D

6. B
7. D
8. C
9. C
10. C

11. D
12. C
13. A
14. C
15. C

16. C
17. A
18. A
19. C
20. C

21. A
22. C
23. C
24. C
25. C

TEST 3

DIRECTIONS: Each question or incomplete statement is followed by several suggested answers or completions. Select the one that BEST answers the question or completes the statement. *PRINT THE LETTER OF THE CORRECT ANSWER IN THE SPACE AT THE RIGHT.*

1. Proteins of superior quality are 1.____
    - A. meats, eggs, milk
    - B. meats, groats, beans
    - C. rice, beans, eggs
    - D. samp, milk, eggs

2. Proteins are classified according to the contained amount of 2.____
    - A. carbon
    - B. purins
    - C. amino acids
    - D. oxygen

3. MOST economic for protein reinforcement of the diet is 3.____
    - A. skim milk powder
    - B. egg yolk
    - C. ice cream
    - D. cream cheese

4. The addition of sodium bicarbonate when cooking green vegetables 4.____
    - A. lowers the boiling point
    - B. improves the taste
    - C. reduces the vitamin content
    - D. inhibits digestion

5. Poor diet may influence the occurrence of 5.____
    - A. cancer
    - B. apoplexy
    - C. metabolic difficulties
    - D. flow of bile

6. Diet therapy is concerned PRINCIPALLY with 6.____
    - A. reducing fat intake
    - B. stimulating impaired tissues
    - C. modifying the usual diet of the patient
    - D. increasing protein intake

7. The BEST dessert to provide additional protein for a meal is 7.____
    - A. apple pie
    - B. fruit jello
    - C. baked custard
    - D. apricot whip

8. To assure adequate nutrition for the aged, provide 8.____
    - A. excess minerals and vitamins
    - B. a standard general diet
    - C. a 4-year-old child's diet
    - D. adequate quantities of food

9. The diet of a 72-year-old obese woman should include extra quantities of 9.____
    - A. proteins
    - B. minerals
    - C. vitamins
    - D. carbohydrates

10. Carbohydrates are stored in the liver in the form of

   A. maltose   B. dextrose   C. glycogen   D. glucose

11. The ONLY source of nitrogen in the diet is

   A. carbohydrates
   B. fat
   C. protein
   D. minerals

12. Some carbohydrates are necessary in a diabetic diet in order that

   A. sugars may be avoided
   B. fats may be oxidized
   C. loss of weight may be prevented
   D. intestinal putrefaction may be reduced

13. A food that is HIGH in essential fatty acids is

   A. heavy cream
   B. halibut
   C. duck
   D. salmon

14. The caloric value of proteins per gram is

   A. 4   B. 3   C. 6   D. 9

15. Low sodium diets are used for

   A. prevention of edema
   B. treatment of diabetes
   C. reduction of cholesterol in the blood
   D. treatment of bacterial endocarditis

16. The rice diet useful in the treatment of hypertensive vascular disease is known by the name of

   A. Kempner   B. Flexner   C. Fleming   D. Harding

17. Pasteurization of milk

   A. reduces the ascorbic acid content
   B. increases the ascorbic acid content
   C. destroys all bacteria
   D. decreases digestibility

18. Among the following, the group of foods which leave an acid ash in the body is

   A. meats, fish, poultry
   B. fruits, milk, vegetables
   C. green vegetables, sugars
   D. pastries, fats, fruits

19. The rate of oxidation of ascorbic acid is reduced by

   A. heat
   B. cold
   C. solution with an alkali
   D. exposure to light

20. The diet which emphasizes frequent small feedings of milk and cream alternating with alkaline powders is called the

   A. Banting
   B. Meniere
   C. Sippy
   D. anti-atherogenic

21. Vitamin A is contained in

    A. animal tissues and in green yellow vegetables
    B. animal tissues and in plants
    C. plants containing carotene
    D. animal tissues

22. Commonly lacking in the diet of teenage girls are

    A. sodium and copper
    B. vitamin B_{12} and D
    C. iron and calcium
    D. vitamin B_1 and riboflavin

23. Low in unsaturated fats is

    A. olive oil
    B. soybean oil
    C. tallow
    D. cottonseed oil

24. A member of the B-complex which promotes iron metabolism is

    A. thiamine
    B. folic acid
    C. niacin
    D. pyridoxin

25. Reduction in incidence of nausea and vomiting during pregnancy has been ascribed to an increase in

    A. B-complex vitamins
    B. ascorbic acid
    C. vitamin D
    D. minerals

KEY (CORRECT ANSWERS)

1.	A	11.	C
2.	C	12.	B
3.	A	13.	C
4.	C	14.	A
5.	C	15.	A
6.	C	16.	A
7.	C	17.	A
8.	C	18.	A
9.	C	19.	B
10.	C	20.	C

21. C
22. C
23. C
24. B
25. A

TEST 4

DIRECTIONS: Each question or incomplete statement is followed by several suggested answers or completions. Select the one that BEST answers the question or completes the statement. *PRINT THE LETTER OF THE CORRECT ANSWER IN THE SPACE AT THE RIGHT.*

1. The four nutritionally important minerals are iron, 1.____

    A. iodine, potassium, and calcium
    B. iodine, phosphorus, and calcium
    C. potassium, phosphorus, and calcium
    D. iodine, sulphur, and calcium

2. Normal peristalsis in the digestive tract is encouraged by 2.____

    A. niacin   B. vitamin A
    C. thiamine   D. ascorbic acid

3. A MAIN source of riboflavin is 3.____

    A. meat   B. whole grains
    C. fruits and vegetables   D. milk

4. Invert sugar is a mixture of equal parts of 4.____

    A. lactose and maltose   B. fructose and lactose
    C. fructose and glucose   D. maltose and glucose

5. Whole grain products differ from *enriched* products in possessing a greater content of 5.____

    A. niacin   B. carbohydrates
    C. riboflavin   D. protein

6. Nutritionists recommend that our yearly per capita intake of sugar be reduced from 100 pounds to 6.____

    A. 65   B. 50   C. 35   D. 20

7. Proteins are 7.____

    A. capable of precipitating copper in Fehling's solution
    B. chemically insolvent
    C. substitutes for starch in body functions
    D. precursors of body catalysts

8. An inexpensive source of vitamin C is 8.____

    A. cabbage   B. asparagus   C. broccoli   D. cucumbers

9. In international units per pound, the United States Department of Agriculture standard for vitamin A fortification of margarine is 9.____

    A. 15,000   B. 5,000   C. 9,000   D. 25,000

10. The vitamin C content of 1 cup of pineapple juice is equivalent to that found in _____ cup of orange juice.

    A. 1 B. 3/4 C. 1/2 D. 1/4

11. Pellagra indicates a deficiency of

    A. ascorbic acid B. niacin
    C. thiamine D. riboflavin

12. Provitamin A is

    A. ergosterol B. carotene
    C. lysine D. pyrodoxine

13. A characteristic of riboflavin deficiency is

    A. cheilosis B. catarrh C. otitis D. pellagra

14. In anabolism, the number of calories yielded by one gram of carbohydrates is

    A. two B. four C. six D. eight

15. Cheese is rich in

    A. calcium B. iron C. sodium D. potassium

16. Whole grain products, in contrast with enriched products, possess more

    A. hydrocarbons B. carbohydrates
    C. vitamins D. proteins

17. The nutritionally important minerals are

    A. sodium, iodine, potassium, copper
    B. iron, iodine, phosphorus, calcium
    C. iron, potassium, sulphur, copper
    D. sodium, phosphorus, sulphur, calcium

18. Contributing MOST to the weight of the living human body is

    A. copper B. sodium C. calcium D. iron

19. The item that acts as a catalytic agent for the assimilation of calcium and phosphorus is

    A. vitamin D B. fat
    C. vitamin C D. protein

20. RICHEST vitamin D food for a one-year-old child is

    A. egg yolk B. homogenized milk
    C. spinach D. cod liver oil

21. Vitamin A is used in the body to

    A. stimulate the appetite B. maintain nerve tissue
    C. resist infection D. grow bone

22. Vitamin A is MOST concentrated in

    A. cream   B. whole milk
    C. skim milk   D. certified milk

23. HIGHEST in vitamin C is

    A. egg yolk   B. soft-cooked egg
    C. beef juice   D. tomato juice

24. Vitamins are lacking in

    A. butter   B. fruit   C. egg   D. sugar

25. The oil RICHEST in vitamin D is

    A. mineral oil   B. olive oil
    C. crisco   D. cod liver oil

KEY (CORRECT ANSWERS)

1.	C	11.	B
2.	C	12.	B
3.	D	13.	A
4.	C	14.	B
5.	A	15.	A
6.	B	16.	D
7.	D	17.	B
8.	A	18.	C
9.	A	19.	A
10.	C	20.	D

21. C
22. A
23. D
24. D
25. D

TEST 5

DIRECTIONS: Each question or incomplete statement is followed by several suggested answers or completions. Select the one that BEST answers the question or completes the statement. *PRINT THE LETTER OF THE CORRECT ANSWER IN THE SPACE AT THE RIGHT.*

1. To increase vitamin A in the diet, eat 1.____

   A. cream cheese with chopped nuts on whole wheat toast
   B. tuna fish and celery on enriched white toast
   C. chicken and celery on rye bread
   D. shredded carrot and pineapple on white bread

2. Of the following, the process which adds NO food value to milk is 2.____

   A. irradiation   B. condensation with sugar
   C. fortification   D. homogenization

3. Hot, home-prepared cereals, as compared with dry cereals, 3.____

   A. provide more energy   B. cost less
   C. contain more minerals   D. contain more vitamins

4. Puréed fruits and vegetables are served during convalescence because they 4.____

   A. require no chewing
   B. are highly nutritive
   C. do not irritate the digestive tract
   D. appeal to the appetite

5. Of the following, the BEST for growth and general health is 5.____

   A. orange juice, oatmeal, buttered toast, coffee
   B. roll with butter, eggs, coffee
   C. cornflakes, fried eggs, muffins, milk
   D. pancakes, syrup, bacon, milk

6. In wheat, the vitamin B complex is in the 6.____

   A. endosperm   B. aleuron layer
   C. bran   D. germ

7. The duration of infectious colds has been materially diminished by dosages of vitamin 7.____

   A. A   B. B_1 C. B2   D. E

8. A MAJOR source of riboflavin is 8.____

   A. meat   B. whole grains
   C. fruits   D. milk

9. Rich in thiamine is 9.____

   A. orange juice   B. cheese
   C. polished rice   D. brewer's yeast

10. The antihemorrhagic is

    A. riboflavin   B. vitamin A
    C. vitamin K   D. niacin

11. Anemia responds to

    A. ascorbic acid   B. folic acid
    C. niacin   D. carotene

12. Legumes and nuts provide much

    A. thiamine   B. calcium   C. niacin   D. sodium

13. MOST of the body's vitamin A is in the

    A. lungs   B. kidneys   C. liver   D. muscles

14. A food rich in vitamin C is

    A. plums   B. celery
    C. green pepper   D. watermelon

15. The duration of infectious colds has been measurably diminished by administering additional amounts of vitamin

    A. A   B. B_1 C. B_2 D. E

16. Carbohydrate stored in the liver is

    A. galleass   B. glycogen   C. heptarch   D. galactose

17. A quart of milk provides an amount of riboflavin equal to that supplied by lean meat weighing _____ pound(s).

    A. 1/2   B. 1   C. 2   D. 3

18. Provitamin A is

    A. ergosterol   B. carotene
    C. lysine   D. pyrodoxine

19. A person's weight stays the same if he

    A. eats only enough to supply the energy he uses
    B. exercises daily
    C. rests more
    D. eats more fruits and vegetables

20. Enriched white flour contains

    A. niacin, thiamine, and iron
    B. ascorbic acid and vitamin D
    C. vitamin A and niacinamide
    D. folic acid

21. Pellagra is caused by

    A. bacteria   B. deficiency of niacin
    C. deficiency of iron   D. a virus

22. To preserve vitamin C in cooking frozen vegetables,　　　　　　　　　　　　　　　　22._____
    A. cook before thawing in a small amount of boiling water
    B. thaw first and cook quickly
    C. thaw and cook in a small amount of water
    D. keep just below boiling point

23. Calcium and phosphorus are catalytic agents for use of　　　　　　　　　　　　　　　23._____
    A. vitamin D　　　　　　　　　　　　B. fat
    C. vitamin C　　　　　　　　　　　　D. protein

24. Thiamine is found in　　　　　　　　　　　　　　　　　　　　　　　　　　　　　　　24._____
    A. macaroni　　　B. rice　　　　C. pork　　　　D. suet

25. The PRINCIPAL food source of calcium is　　　　　　　　　　　　　　　　　　　　　　25._____
    A. meats　　　　　　　　　　　　　　B. nuts
    C. milk and milk products　　　　　　D. vegetables

KEY (CORRECT ANSWERS)

1.	D	11.	B
2.	D	12.	A
3.	B	13.	C
4.	C	14.	C
5.	A	15.	A
6.	D	16.	B
7.	A	17.	C
8.	D	18.	B
9.	D	19.	A
10.	C	20.	A

21. B
22. A
23. A
24. C
25. C

EXAMINATION SECTION
TEST 1

DIRECTIONS: Each question or incomplete statement is followed by several suggested answers or completions. Select the one that BEST answers the question or completes the statement. *PRINT THE LETTER OF THE CORRECT ANSWER IN THE SPACE AT THE RIGHT.*

1. The one of the following which is the MOST important requirement of a good menu is that it

    A. include a large variety of food
    B. list foods which are well-liked
    C. be printed neatly on a clean menu card
    D. be suited to the purpose for which it is planned

    1.____

2. Of the following, the procedure which is MOST desirable for proper tray service is to

    A. heat all dishes before placing them on the tray
    B. serve hot food hot, and cold food cold
    C. have all patients elevated in order to permit easier swallowing of food
    D. always serve iced water on the tray

    2.____

3. The PROPER position for the knife on the tray is

    A. above the dinner plate
    B. across the bread and butter plate
    C. to the right of the dinner plate
    D. next to the fork

    3.____

4. For attractive tray service, it is MOST advisable to serve harvard beets

    A. on the plate with the meat
    B. in a small side vegetable dish
    C. on a bed of shredded lettuce
    D. with a very thick, heavy sauce

    4.____

5. The kitchen dietitian can work MOST efficiently if her office is located

    A. away from the kitchen, so she can be free from distractions
    B. in a central position where she may view all that happens
    C. at the entrance to the kitchen where she can see people entering and leaving
    D. next to the pantry, so she can see that no unauthorized person enters

    5.____

6. The PRIMARY purpose of keeping records in the dietary department is to

    A. reduce waste in ordering food and supplies
    B. increase consumption of the most nutritious foods
    C. train subordinates in office techniques
    D. maintain statistical records of retail prices

    6.____

41

7. A budget is BEST described as a(n)

   A. detailed plan for expenditures
   B. schedule for figuring depreciation of equipment over a period of years
   C. order for necessary equipment
   D. periodic accounting for past expenditures

8. Of the following, the CHIEF reason why a refrigerator door should NOT be left open is that the open door will

   A. stop the motor
   B. cause a drop in room temperature
   C. permit the cold air to rise to the top
   D. permit warm air to enter the refrigerator

9. Ovens with thermostatic heat controls should be

   A. kept closed at all times
   B. opened carefully to prevent jarring
   C. checked periodically for accuracy
   D. disconnected when not in use

10. The term *net weight* means MOST NEARLY the

    A. actual weight of an item
    B. weight of the container when empty
    C. combined weight of an item and its container
    D. estimated weight of the container alone

11. In requisitioning food, it is LEAST necessary for a dietitian to

    A. specify the exact quantity desired
    B. secure the signature of the cashier
    C. know the delivery times and order accordingly
    D. know the sizes in which foods are marketed

12. When receiving an order of food, it is INADVISABLE for the dietitian to

    A. check carefully against the order or requisition
    B. see that all fresh foods are weighed and checked in at the receiving room
    C. check for quality as well as quantity of foods delivered
    D. subtract two pounds tare from the weight of each package delivered in an order

13. Assume that, when inspecting a delivery of vegetables, you find a large amount of sorrel mixed in with a bushel of spinach.
    The one of the following actions which it is MOST advisable for you to take is to

    A. sort the spinach and sorrel in cleaning and cook them separately to allow greater variety in the menu
    B. discard the sorrel as waste
    C. call the purchasing office and arrange to return the spinach as unsatisfactory
    D. place the sorrel in the refrigerator and return it to the driver on his next delivery

14. When purchasing iceberg lettuce, it is ADVISABLE to look for lettuce which is   14.____

    A. loosely headed, with soft curly leaves and a yellow heart
    B. tightly headed, elongated, with coarse green leaves
    C. tightly headed, with medium green outside leaves and a pale green heart
    D. loosely headed, with elongated stalk and rugged curly leaves

15. The term *30-40 prunes* is used to describe the   15.____

    A. number of prunes in a box
    B. particular variety of prunes
    C. brand name of prunes
    D. number of prunes in a pound

16. When ordering chocolate liquor, the dietitian should expect to receive a _____ choco-   16.____
    late.

    A. solid piece of   B. semi-liquid
    C. liquid   D. glass jar of

17. Of the following, the BEST reason for discarding the green part of potatoes is that it con-   17.____
    tains a poison known as

    A. cevitamic acid   B. citric acid
    C. solanine   D. trichinae

18. The number of cans that a standard case of #10 canned apples USUALLY contains is   18.____

    A. 6   B. 12   C. 18   D. 24

19. Of the following, the person MOST closely associated with work in the field of infant   19.____
    behavior and feeding is

    A. H. Pollack   B. A. Gesell
    C. E.J. Stieglitz   D. J.F. Freeman

20. Of the following, the person BEST known for work in the field of diabetes is   20.____

    A. N. Jolliffe   B. H. Sherman
    C. R.M. Wilder   D. F. Stern

21. An egg which is strictly fresh will   21.____

    A. float in cold water
    B. have a thin and watery egg white
    C. have a swollen egg yolk which is easily broken
    D. sink in cold water

22. Cocoa and chocolate are rich in   22.____

    A. glycogen   B. gum   C. cellulose   D. starch

23. The percentage of protein that is usually converted into glucose in the body is MOST   23.____
    NEARLY

    A. 49%   B. 58%   C. 67%   D. 78%

24. Of the following vegetables, the one which gives the LARGEST yield, pound for pound, when pureed is

    A. fresh celery
    B. frozen peas
    C. frozen asparagus
    D. fresh carrots

24.____

25. If the composition of two small rib chops is Protein - 21 grams and Fat - 17 grams, the number of calories in the two chops is MOST NEARLY

    A. 136   B. 200   C. 237   D. 257

25.____

KEY (CORRECT ANSWERS)

1.	D	11.	B
2.	B	12.	D
3.	C	13.	C
4.	B	14.	C
5.	B	15.	D
6.	A	16.	C
7.	A	17.	C
8.	D	18.	A
9.	C	19.	B
10.	A	20.	C

21. D
22. D
23. B
24. D
25. C

TEST 2

DIRECTIONS: Each question or incomplete statement is followed by several suggested answers or completions. Select the one that BEST answers the question or completes the statement. PRINT THE LETTER OF THE CORRECT ANSWER IN THE SPACE AT THE RIGHT.

1. An APPROPRIATE substitute for sucrose for a patient on a low carbohydrate diet is   1.____
   A. saccharin   B. casec   C. lactose   D. protinol

2. Of the following, the vegetables which are high in protein and, therefore, sometimes substituted for meat are   2.____
   A. green leafy vegetables   B. legumes
   C. root vegetables   D. gourds

3. When planning menus, it is *advisable* to use fish at least once a week because it is a GOOD source of   3.____
   A. iron   B. vitamin C   C. zinc   D. iodine

4. Of the following, the one which is a *non-nutritive* beverage is   4.____
   A. clear tea   B. orangeade
   C. oatmeal gruel   D. cream soda

5. Macaroni is *usually* used as a substitute for   5.____
   A. salad   B. meat   C. potato   D. dessert

6. Bread is dextrinized by   6.____
   A. toasting   B. chopping
   C. drying in open air   D. soaking in hot water

7. Baked custard is used on the menu CHIEFLY   7.____
   A. as a source of vitamin C
   B. because of its high protein content
   C. to add color
   D. as a source of starch

8. The one of the following which is a *non-irritating* food is   8.____
   A. cabbage   B. pickles   C. spaghetti   D. celery

9. Leaves of rhubarb and beets, when boiled in an aluminum container, will clean the container because they contain   9.____
   A. sulphuric acid   B. oxalic acid
   C. ammonia   D. alkali

10. When refinishing a refrigerator ice cube tray, the one of the following which should NOT be used as a coating material is   10.____
    A. aluminum   B. cadmium   C. tin   D. nickel

45

11. The Department of Health requires the sterilization of eating utensils by 11.____

    A. hot air sterilizers
    B. ultraviolet rays
    C. chemical solutions
    D. water at 180° F

12. Suppose that the dishwashing machine has become clogged with food particles. 12.____
    Of the following, the action which would be MOST advisable for the dietitian to take *first* is to

    A. call the service man to disassemble and clean the machine
    B. instruct the employees assigned to washing dishes about proper scraping of dishes
    C. order the employees to prerinse all dishes in order to prevent clogging
    D. remove the strainer tray

13. The one of the following which is the MOST effective way to rid a food storeroom of mice is to 13.____

    A. cement tight all holes which permit invasion
    B. set traps to catch the mice
    C. spread poison around the floor
    D. burn a sulphur candle in the storeroom

14. Black stoves are cleaned BEST by 14.____

    A. polishing with an oiled cloth
    B. rubbing with a piece of wax paper
    C. scrubbing with soap and water
    D. heating until they are red hot

15. Of the following, the BEST procedure for cleaning a red quarry tile floor in a hospital kitchen is to 15.____

    A. scrub it, then wax the floor
    B. hose it down with steam
    C. wash it with a strong soap
    D. wash it with a lye

16. After making ice cream, it is MOST important that the machine be 16.____

    A. rinsed thoroughly in cold water
    B. sterilized
    C. soaked in soap solution
    D. scrubbed with a brush

17. A dietitian assigned to work with clinic patients should have a basic knowledge of the foods of foreign-born people. 17.____
    Of the following, the MOST important reason for this is that

    A. it is interesting and exciting to eat the exotic dishes of foreign lands
    B. such knowledge would prove beyond doubt that poor diet is the cause of poor health among the foreign-born

C. such knowledge would help the dietitian to plan the patient's prescribed diet around familiar foods
D. many foreign dishes are more nutritious than American foods

18. The clinic dietitian meets several problems of the aging. The one of the following for which she is LEAST responsible is the

    A. detection of the onset of chronic degenerative diseases
    B. conservation of the health of the individual
    C. re-evaluation of the caloric requirements of aged patients
    D. overcoming of superstitions and food fallacies

19. When advising on methods of economizing, the clinic dietitian should instruct patients to AVOID buying

    A. foods in quantity, even though storage space permits
    B. foods that are in season and in abundance on the market
    C. less expensive cuts of meat
    D. butter, since there are less expensive substitutes on the market

20. The one of the following services which is the LEAST basic function of a nutrition clinic is to

    A. serve as a teaching center for students
    B. provide educational programs for patients of all ages
    C. follow up the nutritional status of individual patients
    D. secure diet histories of patients for the correction of undesirable food habits

21. Time and motion studies in the field of dietetics are used PRIMARILY to

    A. check on lateness and absence records of employees
    B. reduce effort and increase efficiency in performing particular tasks
    C. prepare estimates of time required between requisition and delivery dates
    D. schedule the daily work assignments for the entire staff

22. The PRIMARY purpose of using standardized recipes is to

    A. aid in controlling food costs
    B. encourage the cooks to try out new foods
    C. prepare large quantities of food
    D. determine the caloric values of foods

23. The CHIEF advantage of keeping a perpetual inventory of stock items is that

    A. supplies may be stored more easily
    B. there will be less breakage and loss of stock
    C. it makes it unnecessary to order replacements for stock supplies
    D. the balance on hand at any time is easily determined

24. In order to prevent the loss of vitamins in cooking, it is HOST advisable to

    A. cover the food completely with water while cooking and boil it rapidly
    B. peel and soak vegetables in cold water before cooking

C. dice vegetables into small pieces and boil them in an open pot
D. cook vegetables in the shortest possible time in a covered pot containing little water

25. To marinate is to

A. let foods stand in a specially prepared liquid to add flavor or to tenderize them
B. cook food in liquid just below the boiling point
C. moisten food while cooking by pouring over it drippings or other liquids
D. cook food in water at boiling temperature

KEY (CORRECT ANSWERS)

1. A
2. B
3. D
4. A
5. C

6. A
7. B
8. C
9. B
10. B

11. D
12. A
13. A
14. C
15. B

16. B
17. C
18. A
19. D
20. A

21. B
22. A
23. D
24. D
25. A

EXAMINATION SECTION
TEST 1

DIRECTIONS: Each question or incomplete statement is followed by several suggested answers or completions. Select the one that BEST answers the question or completes the statement. *PRINT THE LETTER OF THE CORRECT ANSWER IN THE SPACE AT THE RIGHT.*

1. Foods which are left over may be used by the menu planner CHIEFLY to　　　　1.____

    A. baste meats
    B. stock the freezer with emergency supplies
    C. provide more variety in the next day's menu
    D. add minerals to the diet

2. When a recipe calls for cooking in a hot oven, it is MOST desirable to set the thermostat at a Fahrenheit temperature of　　　　2.____

    A. 300°　　　B. 350°　　　C. 425°　　　D. 525°

3. Of the following, the MOST satisfactory method for cooking the less tender cuts of meat is by　　　　3.____

    A. roasting　　　B. broiling　　　C. dry heat　　　D. moist heat

4. A two-pound chicken is BEST prepared by　　　　4.____

    A. broiling　　　B. stewing　　　C. baking　　　D. roasting

5. Fats are used in food preparation, *not only* as emulsifiers, *but also* as　　　　5.____

    A. shortening agents
    B. leavening agents
    C. catalysts
    D. sweetening agents

6. Baking powder is used in cake mixtures CHIEFLY in order to　　　　6.____

    A. improve the flavor
    B. increase the acidity
    C. lighten the cake and increase its volume
    D. hold the other ingredients together

7. When making a sponge cake, it is important to remember to　　　　7.____

    A. beat the batter until it doubles in bulk
    B. bake the cake in an ungreased tube pan
    C. bake the cake in a hot oven
    D. remove the cake from the pan as soon as it is baked

8. When making pastry, the fat should be　　　　8.____

    A. creamed with the flour
    B. first melted and then creamed with the flour
    C. cut into the flour
    D. added to the flour after the water is stirred in

9. Of the following, the procedure which is MOST advisable when cooking dried prunes is to

   A. soak the fruit in hot water to seal in the juices
   B. keep the uncooked fruit under refrigeration at all times
   C. simmer the fruit slowly until it is tender
   D. add sugar to the fruit to improve the flavor

10. Assume that you plan to serve a gelatin dessert for dinner. You have found that gelatin made in the usual way softens in hot weather.
    Of the following, the procedure which is MOST advisable to follow on a warm day is to

    A. thicken the gelatin with cornstarch
    B. substitute a non-gelatin dessert
    C. use fruit juice in the mixture
    D. use less water than usual

11. When preparing cream of tomato soup, it is MOST advisable to

    A. add hot milk slowly to cold tomato juice
    B. mix milk and tomato juice and then heat
    C. add cold tomato juice slowly to hot milk
    D. add cold milk slowly to hot tomato juice

12. In order to prevent cornstarch from lumping in cooking, it is MOST advisable to

    A. mix the starch with cold liquid before heating
    B. add hot liquid immediately to the starch
    C. brown the starch and add hot liquid
    D. heat the starch in a double boiler

13. Of the following, the LEAST desirable way to dry bread is to place it in

    A. uncovered pans on top of heated ovens
    B. paper bags which are suspended over the stoves
    C. deep pans in a warm oven
    D. cabinets which have slow heat

14. Of the following, the one which is a mollusk used in the preparation of soup is

    A. crab   B. oyster   C. lobster   D. cod

15. Whole dry milk is preferable to evaporated milk for use as a beverage CHIEFLY because it

    A. takes less time to prepare
    B. contains more vitamins
    C. can be made to look and taste more like whole milk
    D. contains more calories

16. The one of the following which is a RESIDUE-FREE food is

    A. milk   B. grapefruit sections
    C. lettuce   D. lemon gelatin

17. The one of the following which is NOT a legume is

    A. peanuts   B. okra   C. beans   D. lentils

18. Of the following, the sugar which is SWEETEST is

    A. lactose   B. fructose   C. sucrose   D. maltose

19. Broths are of value in the diet CHIEFLY because they are

    A. high in food value
    B. a good source of protein
    C. effective appetite stimulants
    D. a good source of carbohydrates

20. Of the following groups, the one which may be served on a SOFT diet is

    A. cream soup, mashed potato, spinach puree, toast, butter, custard
    B. broiled chicken, mashed potato, buttered peas, toast, milk
    C. vegetable soup, lamp chops, mashed potato, lettuce salad, toast
    D. clear broth, baked potato, tenderloin steak, carrots, apple pie

21. Of the following fruits, those which may be included in a HIGH ACID ash diet are

    A. prunes   B. oranges   C. bananas   D. pears

22. Of the following statements regarding yeast, the one which is MOST accurate is that yeast

    A. is generally harmful
    B. changes starch to sugar
    C. lives without air
    D. requires alcohol to live

23. The souring of milk is due PRIMARILY to the action of bacteria on

    A. fatty acids   B. proteins   C. amino acids   D. lactose

24. Glycerol, which is an end product of fat metabolism, is further oxidized in the body to

    A. sucrose   B. galactose   C. levulose   D. glucose

25. Cereals should be included in menus that are planned PRIMARILY to be

    A. weight reducing
    B. low in starch
    C. low in cost
    D. high in vitamin C

KEY (CORRECT ANSWERS)

1.	C	11.	C
2.	C	12.	A
3.	D	13.	A
4.	A	14.	B
5.	A	15.	C
6.	C	16.	D
7.	B	17.	B
8.	C	18.	B
9.	C	19.	C
10.	D	20.	A

21. A
22. B
23. D
24. D
25. C

TEST 2

DIRECTIONS: Each question or incomplete statement is followed by several suggested answers or completions. Select the one that BEST answers the question or completes the statement. *PRINT THE LETTER OF THE CORRECT ANSWER IN THE SPACE AT THE RIGHT.*

1. Of the following, a high blood sugar content is MOST likely to be a symptom of

   A. anemia
   B. diabetes mellitus
   C. arteriosclerosis
   D. hypertension

2. Trichinosis is a disease which may be caused by

   A. eating ham which has been overcooked
   B. unsanitary handling of frozen meats
   C. eating food which has been contaminated by infected flies
   D. eating infected pork which has been cooked insufficiently

3. Of the following, the bacteria which causes MOST food poisoning cases is

   A. botulinum   B. salmonella   C. pneumococci   D. streptococci

4. In the normal diet, liver should be used at least once a week since it is a GOOD source of

   A. vitamin C   B. phosphorus   C. iron   D. roughage

5. Water is important in the daily intake of the body CHIEFLY because it

   A. causes the oxidation of food in the body
   B. is a transporting medium for all body substances
   C. cools the air in the lungs
   D. gives off minerals when it is digested

6. Cod liver oil is given to children CHIEFLY in order to aid in

   A. absorption of calcium
   B. carbohydrate metabolism
   C. prevention of beriberi
   D. regulation of osmotic pressure

7. Of the following statements with respect to the nutritional needs of children, the one which is MOST accurate is that

   A. a child of four years of age requires a minimum of 2000 calories a day
   B. it is better for a child to be slightly underweight than to be overweight
   C. proportionately, children require more protein per pound of body weight than do adults
   D. a child whose diet is deficient in vitamin D may develop scurvy as a result

8. The one of the following desserts which it is MOST advisable to use in a low protein diet is

   A. rune soufflé
   B. fruit cup
   C. gelatin
   D. junket

9. The Karell diet is used in the care of

   A. Addison's disease
   B. cardiac conditions
   C. diabetes
   D. jaundice

10. Rowe elimination diets are used in cases involving

    A. allergy
    B. lead poisoning
    C. constipation
    D. nephritis

11. Of the following conditions, the one for which the normal diet is MODIFIED by restricting sodium is

    A. tuberculosis   B. diabetes   C. gastritis   D. edema

12. The one of the following conditions which may cause jaundice is

    A. faulty functioning of the kidneys
    B. an obstruction in the common bile duct
    C. a deficiency of vitamin C
    D. the presence of the yeast spore

13. It is GENERALLY accepted that exophthalmic goiter may result from

    A. the inability of the body to metabolize purines
    B. injury to the pancreas
    C. a diet deficient in iodine
    D. lack of sufficient sunlight and milk

14. Faulty ossification of the legs, ribs, and cranial bones are symptoms GENERALLY associated with

    A. pellagra   B. rickets   C. neuritis   D. encephalitis

15. Of the following diseases, the one which is characterized PRIMARILY by destruction of the liver cells is

    A. diabetes   B. leukemia   C. scurvy   D. cirrhosis

Questions 16-25.

DIRECTIONS: Column I lists 10 diseases or conditions, numbered 16 to 25, which require dietary treatment. Column II lists the dietary treatments which are generally used for the conditions listed in Column I. In the space at the right, opposite the number preceding each of the conditions in Column I, place the letter preceding the dietary treatment in Column II which is MOST appropriate for the condition in Column I.

COLUMN I

16. Addison's disease
17. cirrhosis
18. diabetes
19. exophthalmic goiter
20. gastric ulcer
21. gout
22. lipoid nephrosis
23. obesity
24. rickets
25. typhoid fever

COLUMN II

A. low carbohydrate diet
B. high caloric, non-stimulating diet
C. non-residue diet, high in protein and acid ash
D. diet high in vitamin C and magnesium
E. high protein, high carbohydrate, low roughage diet
F. high caloric, soft diet, given in small, frequent feedings
G. diet high in carbohydrate and vitamins, low in potassium, with added salt
H. diet with normal or high protein, vitamins, and minerals; low in fat and carbohydrate; low in caloric value
I. high protein and sulphur diet
J. low protein, purine-free diet
K. high protein, low fat diet, with limited sodium
L. diet high in protein and carbohydrate, low in fat, high in vitamin B complex
M. diet high in vitamin D

16. _____
17. _____
18. _____
19. _____
20. _____
21. _____
22. _____
23. _____
24. _____
25. _____

KEY (CORRECT ANSWERS)

1. B
2. D
3. B
4. C
5. B

6. A
7. C
8. B
9. B
10. A

11. D
12. B
13. C
14. B
15. D

16. G
17. L
18. A
19. B
20. F

21. J
22. K
23. H
24. M
25. E

EXAMINATION SECTION
TEST 1

DIRECTIONS: Each question or incomplete statement is followed by several suggested answers or completions. Select the one that BEST answers the question or completes the statement. *PRINT THE LETTER OF THE CORRECT ANSWER IN THE SPACE AT THE RIGHT.*

1. The one of the following groups of garnishes or accompaniments which is MOST appropriate for the entree designated is

    A. boiled beef; horseradish sour cream sauce, mixed pickles, beet and onion relish, lemon wedge
    B. roast veal; cranberry sauce, fried apple ring, parsley, French fried onion ring
    C. broiled fish; lemon wedge, tartar sauce, chopped parsley, lemon butter
    D. hamburger; sliced onion, catsup, French fried onion rings, Hollandaise sauce

    1._____

2. Assume that the following menu has been submitted: chicken fricasee, mashed potatoes, cauliflower, bread and butter, applesauce, coffee, tea, milk.
The CHIEF defect of this menu is that it is

    A. inadequate in protein content
    B. lacking in color and texture contrast
    C. improperly balanced as to nutrient content
    D. too high in calories

    2._____

3. Assume that the following menu has been submitted for lunch: baked ham, pan browned parsnips, baked sweet potato, cornbread and butter, Apple Brown Betty with whipped topping.
This menu is NOT well-planned primarily because

    A. there are too many calories
    B. there are no vitamin C foods
    C. there is not enough variety in texture of the foods
    D. the workload is not well distributed for the kitchen's cooking equipment

    3._____

4. If a patient on a diabetic diet dislikes milk, he may exchange the milk with one

    A. bread exchange, one meat exchange, and one fat exchange
    B. fruit exchange
    C. bread exchange, one beverage, and one fat exchange
    D. meat exchange and one fruit exchange

    4._____

5. The one of the following foods which can be used by a diabetic patient as a substitute in a meat exchange is

    A. ice cream
    B. cheddar cheese
    C. lima beans
    D. blackeye peas

    5._____

6. Of the following foods, the one which should NOT be included in a clear liquid diet is

    A. milk
    B. fat-free broth
    C. fruit or vegetable juice
    D. carbonated beverages

    6._____

57

7. The one of the following which is permitted on a 500 mg. sodium diet is

   A. cornflakes
   B. rice krispies
   C. puffed wheat
   D. wheat flakes

8. The one of the following statements which is INCORRECT is that riboflavin

   A. helps the cells utilize oxygen
   B. helps keep vision clear
   C. prevents cracking of mouth corners
   D. helps the body absorb calcium

9. The one of the following which is NOT concerned with the digestion of fat is

   A. cholecystokinin
   B. lipase
   C. bile
   D. ptyalin

10. The diet which should be given to a patient who has chronic kidney disease with nitrogen retention is

    A. high protein, low carbohydrate
    B. low protein
    C. low calcium, low phosphorus
    D. low purine

11. The diet MOST likely to be ordered for the pernicious vomiting of pregnancy is

    A. high carbohydrate, low fat
    B. high carbohydrate, high fat, high protein
    C. low carbohydrate, low fat, high protein
    D. high protein, low sodium

12. In the treatment of hemorrhagic and nutritional anemias, the MOST important nutrients to stress are iron and

    A. protein   B. vitamin A   C. iodine   D. vitamin E

13. The USUAL diet for a patient with acute gallbladder is a _____ diet.

    A. low fat
    B. 1000 mg. sodium
    C. high protein
    D. low cholesterol

14. Assume that a leukemia patient has difficulty swallowing the foods prescribed for her. In order to provide a diet which is nutritionally adequate, it is LEAST advisable to recommend

    A. a liquid diet emphasizing high caloric liquids and protein supplements
    B. nasal tube feeding in order to meet all nutritional requirements and to avoid the problem of swallowing
    C. a diet on which the meat is minced and all fruits and vegetables are pureed
    D. a diet similar to the one prescribed for her except that each item is pureed

15. The diet MOST likely to be prescribed for a patient who has renal stones is a(n) _____ diet.

    A. elimination
    B. low oxalate
    C. low cholesterol
    D. high carbohydrate, low protein, low fat

16. A rice diet is USUALLY prescribed for patients who

   A. have high blood pressure
   B. have a food allergy
   C. are recovering from a gallbladder operation
   D. require a high caloric intake

17. Patients suffering severe burns are MOST likely to have

   A. loss of serum protein   B. steatorrhea
   C. polyneuritis   D. stomatitis

18. Of the following statements concerning phenylketonuria, the one that is NOT correct is that it

   A. is caused by an enzyme deficiency
   B. leads to mental retardation
   C. is treated by the restriction of carbohydrates
   D. must be detected in the first few months of life in order to be treated

19. During all periods of growth, vitamin D is essential for efficient absorption and utilization of

   A. calcium and potassium   B. potassium and iron
   C. magnesium and calcium   D. phosphorus and calcium

20. In the treatment of urinary calculi, the one of the following which will assist in maintaining an acid urine is

   A. cranberry juice   B. peas
   C. cabbage   D. corn oil

21. Of the following, the food containing the HIGHEST amount of thiamine per 100 gram portion is

   A. fresh green peas   B. fresh pork
   C. fresh spinach   D. ground beef

22. The one of the following foods which is the POOREST source of niacin per 100 gram portion is

   A. lean meats   B. peanuts
   C. whole grain cereals   D. green leafy vegetables

23. Of the following lists of foods, the one which will contribute MOST to the ascorbic acid content of a diet is

   A. potatoes, green peppers, raw cabbage
   B. enriched bread, pork, turnips
   C. whole wheat bread, potatoes, prunes
   D. apples, dates, plums

24. Of the following foods, the content of unsaturated fatty acids is GREATEST in

   A. butter   B. corn oil
   C. beef suet   D. lard

25. Of the following, the one with the LOWEST vitamin C content per 4 oz. portion is _____ juice.   25.____

    A. orange
    B. lemon
    C. tomato
    D. grapefruit

KEY (CORRECT ANSWERS)

1.	C	11.	A
2.	B	12.	A
3.	D	13.	A
4.	A	14.	C
5.	B	15.	B
6.	A	16.	A
7.	C	17.	A
8.	D	18.	C
9.	D	19.	D
10.	B	20.	A

21.	B
22.	D
23.	A
24.	B
25.	C

TEST 2

DIRECTIONS: Each question or incomplete statement is followed by several suggested answers or completions. Select the one that BEST answers the question or completes the statement. *PRINT THE LETTER OF THE CORRECT ANSWER IN THE SPACE AT THE RIGHT.*

1. When roasting meat, the GREATEST yield of finished product may be expected when   1._____

    A. it is quickly seared on both sides at the beginning
    B. a high temperature is used throughout the roasting period
    C. a small quantity of water is added during roasting
    D. a low temperature is used throughout the roasting process

2. Of the following, the meat which is LEAST suitable for roasting is   2._____

    A. loin of pork   B. corned brisket
    C. rump of veal   D. leg of lamb

3. The loss of weight which results from braising boneless bottom round of beef, when proper techniques are used, is   3._____

    A. negligible   B. about 10%
    C. about 25%   D. over 50%

4. Of the following, the one which gives the MOST appropriate cooking temperature for the food indicated is   4._____

    A. beef loaf - 450° F   B. baked potatoes - 250° F
    C. caramel custard - 325° F D. gingerbread - 475° F

5. In teaching a *cook trainee* how to deep fat fry various items of food, one should NOT instruct him to   5._____

    A. lower the food into the fat quickly
    B. make uniform portions of food for frying in the same load
    C. fill frying baskets to no more than 2/3 of capacity
    D. drain raw wet foods well before frying

6. Foods cooked incorrectly often lose flavor.
   When cooking beans or carrots, it is LEAST advisable to   6._____

    A. boil them in a small amount of water
    B. cook them in a steamer
    C. cook them in a pressure cooker
    D. cook them in an uncovered kettle

7. Of the following, the one which would make the LEAST satisfactory thickening agent in a casserole is   7._____

    A. wheat flour   B. rice
    C. cornstarch   D. tapioca

8. If baking powder biscuits do not rise to the proper height, the MOST probable cause is too   8._____

    A. *little* shortening   B. *much* handling of dough
    C. *little* flour   D. *much* baking powder

9. A soggy bottom crust in a lemon meringue pie is MOST probably caused by
   A. handling the crust too much
   B. baking at too high a temperature
   C. refrigeration of the crust prior to baking
   D. pouring in the filling when the pie is hot

10. The MOST appropriate type of poultry to purchase for chicken a la king is
    A. fowl   B. roasters   C. fryers   D. broilers

11. Of the following, Grade B eggs may be used MOST satisfactorily for
    A. poaching
    B. scrambling
    C. frying
    D. coddling

12. Considering both quality and economy, the BEST choice of the following grades to be specified when ordering apples for sauce is
    A. fancy
    B. extra fancy
    C. utility
    D. U.S. #1

13. When submitting requisitions, the dietitian should give correct specifications for each item.
    Of the following items, the one which is CORRECTLY specified is
    A. celery - fresh, Grade A, trimmed, in boxes, 140 pounds
    B. oranges - fresh, commercial grade, size 75 to the half crate, 225 pounds
    C. salad greens - romaine, fresh, Grade A, trimmed, 30 pounds
    D. onions - dry, Grade A, in sacks, 200 pounds

14. The one of the following specifications which is INCOMPLETE is
    A. 200 lbs. of ham, 10 to 12 lbs. each, U.S. #1
    B. 120 lbs. fresh bottom rounds, 20 to 30 lbs. each, Choice
    C. 250 lbs. of boneless corned brisket, deckel removed, 10 to 12 lbs. each, Good
    D. 225 lbs. double veal legs, cut short, 40 to 48 lbs. each, Choice

15. Of the following food items, the one which does NOT have the correct varieties listed for it is
    A. melon - Honeydew, Cantaloupe, Persian, Casaba
    B. potatoes - Idaho, Cobbler, Russet, Yam
    C. onions - Spanish, Bermuda, Yellow, Red
    D. apples - McIntosh, Emperor, Delicious, Concord

16. Assume that you plan to serve 500 portions of beef stew, with 3 ounces of cooked meat in each portion.
    To provide this, you would need _____ lbs. _____ beef chuck.
    A. 95; boneless
    B. 100; whole
    C. 125; boneless
    D. 175; whole

17. You are serving buttered carrot rings on a menu for which you need 750 servings. The number of pounds of topped carrots you should order is MOST NEARLY _____ lbs.

    A. 50 B. 75 C. 150 D. 300

18. Frozen broccoli is on the menu for dinner and you require 260 servings. The number of 2 1/2 lb. packages you would need is MOST NEARLY

    A. 10 B. 25 C. 50 D. 100

19. You wish to serve canned peas to 300 patients on the regular diet, 50 patients on bland diet, 35 patients on low fat diet, and 65 patients on light diet. Peas are supplied in #10 cans, and these are ordered by the case only.
    The number of cases you would need is

    A. 1 B. 2 C. 3 D. 4

20. In order to ensure a minimum of leftover when you plan to serve 3 oz. portions of mashed potatoes to 500 persons, it would be BEST to order _____ potatoes.

    A. 40 lbs. instant
    B. 50 lbs. peeled
    C. 2 cases #10 cans of whole
    D. one 100 lb. sack of

21. The one of the following amounts which is MOST likely to yield 100 average servings is

    A. dry prunes, 25 lbs.
    B. bacon, sliced, rind removed (2 slices per serving), 20 lbs.
    C. coffee, ground for drip, percolator or silex, 2 lbs.
    D. egg noodles, buttered, 18 lbs.

22. The one of the following which would be INCORRECT to order when serving 200 persons is

    A. 8 #10 cans of applesauce
    B. 1 1/2 cases of #5 cans of tomato juice
    C. 100 lbs. of eviscerated fowl
    D. 20 lbs. of rice

23. To ensure that foods are relatively free of contamination when served in a cafeteria during a three hour meal period, it would be MOST advisable to

    A. stagger periods of preparation and service to the counter
    B. maintain a steam table temperature of 120° F
    C. reheat foods when they cool down
    D. eliminate all creamed foods from the menu

24. If egg salad has been prepared in a safe and sanitary manner, the criterion to be used to determine if it may be served one day later is that it

    A. still tastes good
    B. has a satisfactory general appearance
    C. still smells good
    D. has been continuously refrigerated

25. The one of the following statements concerning proper storage which is INCORRECT is   25.____
    that
    A. crates of eggs should be stored upright, never on ends or sides, because eggs are packed with the small end down
    B. crates of lettuce or fruit should not be stacked upright but on the side and should be cross-stacked to provide for air circulation
    C. fresh raw meat such as veal carcass should be carefully wrapped when stored to prevent contamination
    D. onions and potatoes do not require refrigeration; they are best stored in a dark, well-ventilated room at a temperature of 50° to 60° F

KEY (CORRECT ANSWERS)

1. D   11. B
2. B   12. C
3. C   13. C
4. C   14. A
5. A   15. D

6. D   16. C
7. C   17. C
8. B   18. B
9. D   19. C
10. A   20. D

21. C
22. D
23. A
24. D
25. C

TEST 3

DIRECTIONS: Each question or incomplete statement is followed by several suggested answers or completions. Select the one that BEST answers the question or completes the statement. *PRINT THE LETTER OF THE CORRECT ANSWER IN THE SPACE AT THE RIGHT.*

1. Of the following, the one which gives the LEAST desirable temperature for storing the item indicated is

    A. ripe bananas - 60° to 70° F
    B. fresh eggs - 53° to 58° F
    C. salad greens - 40° to 45° F
    D. fresh lamb - 33° to 38° F

    1._____

2. Of the following, the MOST important reason for requiring good ventilation in a storeroom is to prevent

    A. condensation of moisture
    B. roach or rodent infestation
    C. complaints from storekeepers about odors
    D. spoilage of canned goods

    2._____

3. Of the following foods, the one which is LEAST susceptible to insect infestation is

    A. dried beans   B. dried fruits
    C. plain gelatin   D. non-fat dry milk

    3._____

4. Of the following, the MOST effective measure for the elimination of rodents in a hospital kitchen is to

    A. clean the floors every day
    B. spread poison once a month in all allowable areas
    C. eliminate harborages
    D. screen off the slop sinks at all times

    4._____

5. Of the following ways to store food, it is LEAST desirable to place

    A. sacks of dried beans on racks
    B. cans of peas on the floor
    C. packages of cereal on shelves
    D. quarters of lamb on hooks in the refrigerator

    5._____

6. The MOST important reason for NOT overcrowding refrigerators is to

    A. make cleaning easier
    B. allow air circulation to reach all foods
    C. prevent waste resulting from overlooked foods
    D. reduce opportunities for pilferage of food

    6._____

7. Cooked foods should be cooled and refrigerated quickly, PRIMARILY to

    A. *prevent* growth and development of bacteria
    B. *preserve* food nutrients

    7._____

C. *prevent* loss of moisture content
D. *preserve* a *fresh cooked* appearance

8. In planning the layout of a kitchen, it is MOST important to arrange for

   A. grouping together of large pieces of equipment
   B. a separate work area for each cook
   C. a smooth and orderly flow of work
   D. separation of *wet* and *dry* areas

9. Of the following, the MOST satisfactory work surface for a cook's work table is

   A. hardwood 4" thick
   B. heavy gauge stainless steel
   C. heavy duty galvanized iron
   D. heavy gauge aluminum

10. Of the following, the practice which is LEAST advisable in the operation and maintenance of a food grinder is to

    A. hold the knife and plate in place by screwing the adjustment ring as tight as possible
    B. use a mallet to push pieces of food into the grinder
    C. remove the grinder plate and clean it thoroughly with a brush after each use
    D. remove the grinder head at the end of the day and clean all loose parts before storing them

11. The MAIN reason for selecting a cafeteria counter of standard fabricated units rather than a custom-built counter of the same quality is the

    A. lower initial cost
    B. easier cleaning
    C. greater flexibility for change and expansion
    D. lower maintenance costs

12. Of the following, the MOST suitable steam equipment for a main kitchen in a 100 bed hospital is

    A. one compartment steamer, one 80 gallon jacketed kettle, and one 60 gallon jacketed kettle
    B. two 30 gallon jacketed kettles and one 20 gallon jacketed kettle
    C. one 3 compartment steamer and two 30 gallon jacketed kettles
    D. two 2 compartment steamers and one 20 gallon jacketed kettle

13. The BEST choice for the top of a kitchen work table is

    A. 2 inch solid wood
    B. 12 gauge monel metal
    C. 20 gauge stainless steel
    D. galvanized metal

14. For equipment such as steam tables which require a water supply, it is MOST important to

    A. make sure there are no submerged inlets
    B. specify all stainless steel construction
    C. provide a heat booster
    D. supply both hot and cold water

15. In requisitioning a steam jacketed kettle, the LEAST important specification is that the

    A. draw off tube should be as close to the kettle as possible
    B. bottom should be pitched to facilitate run-off of contents
    C. kettle should be wall hung for easier cleaning
    D. draw off valve should be easily removable

16. The MAIN factor to consider when purchasing a slicing machine is the

    A. ease of cleaning
    B. adequacy of the safety guard for the cutting edge
    C. size of the machine in relation to the volume of slicing
    D. availability of replacement parts

17. In submitting your annual budget, you have requested a 2 drawer work table of complete stainless steel construction.
    If you are told that you must request a less expensive model, the MOST acceptable compromise for you to make would be to

    A. substitute ducoed legs with stainless steel feet
    B. substitute drawers of galvanized metal with stainless steel fronts
    C. specify a lighter weight stainless steel
    D. reduce the size of the table

18. The one of the following which is MOST likely to yield 100 average servings is

    A. fish filet - 30 pounds
    B. cream for coffee - 6 quarts
    C. oatmeal (rolled oats) - 5 pounds
    D. frozen spinach - 10 pounds

19. The one of the following requisitions which is NOT correct for 600 servings is

    A. 15 lbs. of ground coffee
    B. 9 lbs. of margarine chips for toast
    C. 3 #10 cans of jelly
    D. 60 lbs. of granulated sugar for cereal

20. You have requisitioned 8000 lbs. of beef carcass (650 to 700 lbs. per carcass). This will yield tender steaks, tender roasts, and less tender cuts for roasting, stewing, and chopping.
    Taking into account loss from trim, bones, and fat when the carcasses are processed, the amount of edible meat these carcasses should yield is MOST NEARLY _____ lbs.

    A. 4500   B. 5360   C. 6500   D. 7120

21. Analysis of the distribution of the average food dollar in a hospital can be of assistance to the dietitian in planning for and checking on the expenditure of funds.
    Of the following, the MOST advisable distribution of funds for categories of food is:
    meat, poultry, and fish _____%; dairy products _____%; fruits and vegetables _____%; bread and cereal _____%; miscellaneous _____%.

    A. 40; 20; 20; 10; 10
    B. 50; 10; 10; 10; 20
    C. 20; 20; 20; 20; 20
    D. 30; 30; 30; 5; 5

22. When planning a nutrition curriculum for the clinical instruction of student nurses, the factor which deserves the LEAST consideration is the

    A. educational purposes which the school of nursing seeks to attain
    B. educational experiences which are likely to meet the school's objectives
    C. service needs of the dietary department of the hospital
    D. methods of determining if the educational objectives have been attained

23. The current trend in the teaching of nutrition and diet therapy to student nurses emphasizes

    A. role playing and discussion groups as the most significant teaching devices
    B. instruction in food laboratories on preparation of foods
    C. instruction in food preparation and service to patients in the wards
    D. the clinical importance of diet therapy in a patient-centered plan of teaching

24. Suppose that the electric slicer used in the main kitchen is frequently out of order because of a short in the motor. The repair mechanic has demonstrated that this happens because excessive moisture is being used to flush out debris when cleaning the machine.
    To prevent repetition of this breakdown, it would be MOST advisable to

    A. issue detailed written instructions on maintenance procedures to all cooks and kitchen employees who might have occasion to use or clean this slicer
    B. issue an order to all employees that no water is to
    C. be used when cleaning this slicer, only clean dry rags
    D. replace the slicer with a manual one that does not have a motor and, therefore, does not require electric current
    E. instruct two employees on each shift on the procedures to be used in cleaning the machine and restrict the use of the machine to them

25. Assume that a dietitian had instructed the kitchen helpers on how to minimize waste when preparing food for cooking. It would be MOST reasonable to conclude that such waste had been reduced subsequently if

    A. on a spot check, the employees observed were preparing the food as instructed
    B. operating costs for the dietary division during the next month were reduced
    C. the amount of food prepared during the next month decreased on a per capita basis
    D. requisitions of food supplies during the next month decreased

KEY (CORRECT ANSWERS)

1.	B	11.	C
2.	A	12.	C
3.	C	13.	B
4.	C	14.	A
5.	B	15.	C
6.	B	16.	B
7.	A	17.	A
8.	C	18.	A
9.	B	19.	D
10.	A	20.	B
21.	A		
22.	C		
23.	D		
24.	D		
25.	C		

EXAMINATION SECTION
TEST 1

DIRECTIONS: Each question or incomplete statement is followed by several suggested answers or completions. Select the one that BEST answers the question or completes the statement. *PRINT THE LETTER OF THE CORRECT ANSWER IN THE SPACE AT THE RIGHT.*

1. The item that acts as a catalytic agent for the assimilation of calcium and phosphorus is   1._____

    A. vitamin D   B. fat   C. vitamin B   D. protein

2. Contributing MOST to the weight of the living human body is   2._____

    A. copper   B. sodium   C. calcium   D. iron

3. Before cooking, the vegetable that MUST be soaked in water is   3._____

    A. string beans   B. Brussels sprouts
    C. turnips   D. celery

4. Amino acids are absorbed MAINLY in the   4._____

    A. stomach   B. liver   C. pancreas   D. intestine

5. Little spoilage occurs in stored, sun-dried fruits because the   5._____

    A. microorganisms have been destroyed
    B. moisture content is low
    C. pectin is inactive
    D. yeasts do not flourish in the absence of light

6. In pickling, the concentrated brine   6._____

    A. softens the cellulose
    B. preserves the original color
    C. retards the growth of microorganisms
    D. increases the acid content

7. Cheese is rich in   7._____

    A. calcium   B. iron   C. sodium   D. potassium

8. Tenderized dried fruits have been   8._____

    A. sulphurized, dried, then partially cooked
    B. dried, partially cooked, then partially dried
    C. partially cooked, dried, then partially cooked
    D. dried, sulphurized, then partially cooked

9. The MOST tender cuts of beef are from the   9._____

    A. loin and rib   B. leg and rib
    C. shoulder and loin   D. rump and neck

10. In anabolism, the number of calories yielded by one gram of carbohydrates is

    A. two   B. four   C. six   D. eight

11. When making yeast rolls, the milk is scalded to

    A. improve the flavor of the product
    B. reduce the size of the air holes
    C. destroy the microorganisms
    D. encourage development of the yeast

12. Deterioration of dried vegetables is retarded by

    A. marinating before drying
    B. storage in metal boxes
    C. pre-cooking before drying
    D. infra-red light treatment before packaging

13. The LARGEST percentage of gluten is found in flour made from

    A. rye   B. barley   C. oats   D. wheat

14. A bed roll is a support for the patient's

    A. head   B. knees   C. back   D. feet

15. One pound of dried eggs is equivalent to _____ eggs.

    A. 50-60   B. 30-40   C. 20-25   D. 15-18

16. To store eggs at home,

    A. keep them exposed on the cupboard
    B. wash and place them in the refrigerator
    C. do not wash and place them in the refrigerator
    D. place them in a moderately cool place

17. Disease is MOST commonly spread through

    A. clothing   B. dishes   C. food   D. contact

18. For everyday use, the Fahrenheit temperature of the refrigerator should be

    A. 20°-25°   B. 35°-40°   C. 45°-50°   D. 55°-60°

19. To retard spoilage of bread, baking companies may add sodium

    A. benzoate   B. propionate
    C. sulphathionate   D. hypophosphate

20. Essential to jelly-making is

    A. proto-pectin   B. pectin
    C. pectic acid   D. pectoral liquor

KEY (CORRECT ANSWERS)

1. A
2. C
3. B
4. D
5. B

6. C
7. A
8. B
9. A
10. B

11. D
12. C
13. D
14. B
15. B

16. C
17. D
18. B
19. B
20. B

TEST 2

DIRECTIONS: Each question or incomplete statement is followed by several suggested answers or completions. Select the one that BEST answers the question or completes the statement. *PRINT THE LETTER OF THE CORRECT ANSWER IN THE SPACE AT THE RIGHT.*

1. A MAJOR source of riboflavin is   1._____
   - A. meat
   - B. whole grains
   - C. fruits
   - D. milk

2. In wheat, the vitamin B complex is in the   2._____
   - A. endosperm
   - B. aleuron layer
   - C. bran
   - D. germ

3. The duration of infectious colds has been materially diminished by dosages of vitamin   3._____
   - A. A
   - B. B_1
   - C. B_2
   - D. E

4. Yeast plants grow BEST at the Fahrenheit temperature of   4._____
   - A. 70°-75°
   - B. 80°-85°
   - C. 90°-95°
   - D. 100°-105°

5. A characteristic of riboflavin deficiency is   5._____
   - A. cheilosis
   - B. catarrh
   - C. otitis
   - D. pellagra

6. Anemia responds to   6._____
   - A. ascorbic acid
   - B. folic acid
   - C. niacin
   - D. carotene

7. Legumes and nuts provide much   7._____
   - A. thiamine
   - B. calcium
   - C. niacin
   - D. sodium

8. Rich in thiamine is   8._____
   - A. orange juice
   - B. cheese
   - C. polished rice
   - D. brewer's yeast

9. Carbohydrate stored in the liver is   9._____
   - A. galleasss
   - B. glycogen
   - C. liepstarch
   - D. galactose

10. The antihemmorhagic is   10._____
    - A. riboflavin
    - B. vitamin A
    - C. vitamin K
    - D. niacin

11. At the end of one year, the weight of an infant in relation to its birth weight should be   11._____
    - A. an increase of 12 oz. monthly
    - B. double
    - C. 20 pounds more
    - D. triple

12. Pellagra indicates a deficiency of   12.____

    A. ascorbic acid   B. niacin
    C. thiamine   D. riboflavin

13. Provitamin A is   13.____

    A. ergosterol   B. carotene
    C. lysine   D. pyrodoxine

14. The nutritionally important minerals are   14.____

    A. sodium, iodine, potassium, copper
    B. iron, iodine, phosphorus, calcium
    C. iron, potassium, sulphur, copper
    D. sodium, phosphorus, sulphur, calcium

15. Root vegetables are BEST stored in atmosphere that is maintained   15.____

    A. at 36° F   B. dehumidified
    C. at 30° F   D. at 75% humidity

16. The government stamp on meats indicates   16.____

    A. date when slaughtered   B. point of origin
    C. nutritional value   D. quality

17. Whole grain products, in contrast with enriched products, possess more   17.____

    A. hydrocarbons   B. carbohydrates
    C. vitamins   D. proteins

18. In anabolism, the number of calories yielded by one gram of hydrocarbon is   18.____

    A. six   B. seven   C. eight   D. nine

19. In the digestion of starch, the intermediate product is   19.____

    A. dextrin   B. fibrinogen   C. cerine   D. maltine

20. Egg whites whip more quickly at the Fahrenheit temperature of   20.____

    A. 0°   B. 30°   C. 70°   D. 85°

KEY (CORRECT ANSWERS)

1.	D	11.	D
2.	D	12.	B
3.	A	13.	B
4.	B	14.	B
5.	A	15.	A
6.	B	16.	D
7.	A	17.	D
8.	D	18.	D
9.	B	19.	A
10.	C	20.	C

EXAMINATION SECTION
TEST 1

DIRECTIONS: Each question or incomplete statement is followed by several suggested answers or completions. Select the one that BEST answers the question or completes the statement. *PRINT THE LETTER OF THE CORRECT ANSWER IN THE SPACE AT THE RIGHT.*

1. Spinach should be cooked

    A. in boiling water, without a cover
    B. dry, in an open pot
    C. dry, in a covered pot
    D. in boiling water with a cover

2. For cookies, one may use melted _____ fat.

    A. beef   B. ham   C. chicken   D. lamb

3. Baking powder is used in proportion to the

    A. flour   B. egg   C. liquid   D. shortening

4. To prevent curdling of soft custard, cook

    A. over boiling water
    B. and stir constantly
    C. over a low flame
    D. over water about to boil

5. In dressings, an example of a *permanent emulsion* is

    A. French dressing
    B. mineral oil
    C. mayonnaise dressing
    D. olive oil

6. Eggs stored in the home should be

    A. uncovered in the refrigerator
    B. washed
    C. in a cool place but not in the refrigerator
    D. in a refrigerator in a covered container

7. Meat should be stored in the refrigerator overnight for use on the next day

    A. loosely covered with patapar in the freezing unit
    B. tightly covered with aluminum foil in a cool part
    C. covered with aluminum foil in the freezing unit
    D. loosely covered with wax paper in a cool part

8. The MOST tender cuts of beef come from the

    A. loin and rib
    B. leg and rib
    C. shoulder and loin
    D. rump and neck

9. To preserve vitamin C in cooking frozen vegetables,

    A. cook before thawing in a small amount of boiling water
    B. thaw first and cook quickly

C. thaw and cook in a small amount of water
D. keep just below boiling point

10. Calcium and phosphorus are catalytic agents for use of

    A. vitamin D   B. fat   C. vitamin B   D. protein

11. Yeast plants grow BEST at a temperature of _____ F.

    A. 70°-75°   B. 80°-85°   C. 90°-95°   D. 100°-105°

12. Tunnels in plain muffins are due to

    A. overheating
    B. underbeating
    C. using too much shortening
    D. using too little shortening

13. For each cup of sour milk in a recipe, add soda in the amount of _____ teaspoon(s).

    A. 2   B. 1   C. 1/2   D. 1/4

14. Incompletely cooked pork, if eaten, may result in

    A. botulism   B. ptomaine
    C. trichinosis   D. typhoid

15. In cooked frostings, cream of tartar is added to

    A. provide a tang
    B. accelerate crystallization
    C. minimize the size of crystals
    D. increase viscosity

16. When substituting sodium aluminum sulphate-phosphate baking powder in a recipe calling for a tartrate baking powder, use _____ of the former per cup of flour

    A. one-half as much   B. one-half more
    C. the same amount   D. one-quarter

17. The MOST appropriate poultry to buy for a chicken fricassee is the

    A. broiler   B. guinea hen
    C. capon   D. fowl

18. Artichokes are scarce because they

    A. are in slight demand   B. are difficult to digest
    C. do not keep well   D. require special cultivation

19. Less tender cuts of meat may be tenderized by

    A. quick cooking   B. the addition of tomatoes
    C. pan frying   D. broiling

20. The official grades for canned fruits which have been set up by the U.S. Department of Agriculture are A, (Fancy);

A. B, (Choice); C, (Standard)
B. B, (Choice)
C. B, (Choice); C, (Substandard)
D. C, (Standard)

21. If both starch and egg are used for thickening a mixture, the egg should be 21.____

    A. thoroughly beaten before it is added to the mixture
    B. added to the mixture after the starch is thoroughly cooked
    C. combined with the liquid ingredients
    D. combined with the dry ingredients

22. For everyday use, it is BEST to maintain the temperature of the refrigerator at _____ F. 22.____

    A. 20°-25°   B. 35°-40°   C. 45°-50°   D. 55°-60°

23. As to pork, the federal meat inspection law should be amended to require examination for 23.____

    A. botulism   B. trichina   C. tetanus   D. fastigium

24. When all-purpose flour is used in a recipe calling for pastry flour, for each cup of flour in the recipe _____ tablespoonsful. 24.____

    A. add two   B. subtract two
    C. add one   D. subtract one

25. Federal law regulates foods sold in 25.____

    A. cities   B. rural areas
    C. states   D. interstate commerce

KEY (CORRECT ANSWERS)

1. D   11. D
2. C   12. A
3. A   13. C
4. B   14. C
5. C   15. C

6. D   16. A
7. C   17. A
8. A   18. D
9. A   19. B
10. A   20. A

21. B
22. B
23. B
24. B
25. D

TEST 2

DIRECTIONS: Each question or incomplete statement is followed by several suggested answers or completions. Select the one that BEST answers the question or completes the statement. *PRINT THE LETTER OF THE CORRECT ANSWER IN THE SPACE AT THE RIGHT.*

1. Goiters are caused by lack of

   A. iodine in the food
   B. iron in food
   C. chlorine in the water supply
   D. vitamins in vegetables

   1._____

2. Of the following, the MOST inexpensive source of nutritive food is

   A. soybean   B. cereal   C. eggs   D. meats

   2._____

3. In international units per pound, the vitamin A level of butter is *approximately*

   A. 9,000   B. 15,000   C. 3,000   D. 5,000

   3._____

4. Vitamin A value of carrots is HIGHEST when they are

   A. harvested as baby carrots
   B. harvested later as mature carrots
   C. selected on the basis of variety
   D. planted in rich loam

   4._____

5. Calciferol and viosterol are produced by irradiation of

   A. ergosterol
   B. cholesterol
   C. ascorbic acid
   D. leucosin

   5._____

6. Provitamin A is

   A. ergosterol
   B. carotene
   C. lysine
   D. pyrodoxine

   6._____

7. Breast feeding

   A. is unimportant
   B. is a drain on the mother
   C. increases infant development
   D. provides temporary immunity

   7._____

8. A roast shrinks LEAST if

   A. cooked at 300° - 350° F.
   B. first seared
   C. cooked at 500° F.
   D. cooked in a small amount of water

   8._____

9. When making yeast rolls, the milk is scalded in order to 9.____
   A. improve the flavor of the product
   B. reduce the size of the air holes
   C. destroy microorganisms
   D. encourage the development of yeast

10. When making medium white sauce, the ratio of fat to flour per cup of milk is 10.____
    A. 1 tsp. to 1 tsp.
    B. 2 tbsp. to 2 tbsp.
    C. 1 tbsp. to 1 tbsp.
    D. 1 tbsp. to 2 tbsp.

11. The four nutritionally important minerals are iron, 11.____
    A. iodine, potassium, and calcium
    B. iodine, phosphorus, and calcium
    C. potassium, phosphorus, and calcium
    D. iodine, sulphur, and calcium

12. Normal peristalsis in the digestive tract is encouraged by 12.____
    A. niacin
    B. vitamin A
    C. thiamine
    D. ascorbic acid

13. A MAIN source of riboflavin is 13.____
    A. meat
    B. whole grains
    C. fruits and vegetables
    D. milk

14. Invert sugar is a mixture of equal parts of 14.____
    A. lactose and maltose
    B. fructose and lactose
    C. fructose and glucose
    D. maltose and glucose

15. Whole grain products differ from *enriched* products in possessing a GREATER content of 15.____
    A. niacin
    B. carbohydrates
    C. riboflavin
    D. protein

16. Nutritionists recommend that our yearly per capita intake of sugar be reduced from 100 pounds to 16.____
    A. 65
    B. 50
    C. 35
    D. 20

17. Proteins are 17.____
    A. capable of precipitating copper in Fehling's solution
    B. chemically insolvent
    C. substitutes for starch in body functions
    D. precursors of body catalysts

18. An inexpensive source of vitamin C is 18.____
    A. cabbage
    B. asparagus
    C. broccoli
    D. cucumbers

19. In international units per pound, the U.S. Department of Agriculture standard for vitamin A fortification of margarine is 19.____
    A. 15,000
    B. 5,000
    C. 9,000
    D. 25,000

20. The vitamin C content of one cup of pineapple juice is equivalent to that found in _____ cup of orange juice.
    A. 1
    B. 3/4
    C. 1/2
    D. 1/4

21. Pellagra indicates a deficiency of
    A. ascorbic acid
    B. niacin
    C. thiamine
    D. riboflavin

22. A growing child should NOT drink coffee because it
    A. acts as a stimulant
    B. is habit-forming
    C. reduces milk intake
    D. spoils the appetite

23. The PRINCIPAL food source of calcium is
    A. meats
    B. nuts
    C. milk and milk products
    D. vegetables

24. Legumes and nuts provide a RICH source of
    A. thiamine
    B. calcium
    C. niacin
    D. sodium

25. Since 1850, the per capita consumption of sugar in the United States has increased
    A. 900%
    B. 150%
    C. 500%
    D. 300%

KEY (CORRECT ANSWERS)

1. A	11. C
2. A	12. C
3. B	13. D
4. A	14. C
5. A	15. A
6. B	16. B
7. C	17. D
8. A	18. A
9. B	19. A
10. B	20. C

21. B
22. C
23. C
24. A
25. D

EXAMINATION SECTION
TEST 1

DIRECTIONS: Each question or incomplete statement is followed by several suggested answers or completions. Select the one that BEST answers the question or completes the statement. *PRINT THE LETTER OF THE CORRECT ANSWER IN THE SPACE AT THE RIGHT.*

1. Fuel value of foods is determined by use of a(n)   1._____
   A. caloric unit B. calorific unit
   C. calciferol   D. calorimeter

2. Folacin is necessary for   2._____
   A. digestion of carbohydrates
   B. metabolism of sterols
   C. synthesis of chlorophyll
   D. hematopoiesis

3. Avidin is a(n)   3._____
   A. vitamin   B. protein   C. fiber   D. fabric

4. Baking powders are a mixture of cornstarch, baking soda, and a(n)   4._____
   A. acid   B. alkali   C. gas   D. neutralizer

5. The CORRECT method of cooking green-colored vegetables is to   5._____
   A. pressure cook
   B. add a small amount of baking soda
   C. release the steam occasionally while cooking in a covered saucepan
   D. keep the saucepan tightly covered

6. Popovers and cream puffs are PRINCIPALLY leavened by   6._____
   A. steam   B. air
   C. carbon dioxide D. nitrous oxide

7. Compared with the recommended figure of 50%, the actual percentage of food calories derived from protective foods in the American diet is   7._____
   A. 20%   B. 25%   C. 33%   D. 45%

8. A bacteriostatic method of food preservation is   8._____
   A. open kettle canning   B. pressure canning
   C. dehydration   D. irradiation

9. For the average American, minerals of value as food supplements for the diet are calcium,   9._____
   A. phosphorus, sodium, and choline
   B. chlorine, magnesium, and iron
   C. phosphorus, iron, and iodine
   D. chlorine, iron, and manganese

10. For the average American, the vitamins of value as food supplements are thiamine, pyridoxine, riboflavin, calciferol, ascorbic acid, and

    A. niacin, B_{12}, A
    B. B_6, B_{12}, folic acid
    C. B_{12}, K and A
    D. B_{12}, A and E

11. The critical temperatures for eggs in storage are

    A. 28° and 68°
    B. 32° and 75°
    C. 38° and 60°
    D. 25° and 75°

12. When they are to form an ingredient in cake, eggs blend with the batter better if they are

    A. new laid
    B. chilled thoroughly
    C. brought to room temperature
    D. candled

13. Of the following, the HIGHEST in caloric value is 1 cupful

    A. strained honey
    B. orange juice
    C. sugar
    D. homogenized milk

14. Among the following, the BEST food source of thiamine is

    A. refined sugars
    B. fats
    C. egg white
    D. pork

15. In the list below, the BEST source of vitamin A is

    A. wheat germ   B. pork   C. milk   D. spinach

16. A disadvantage resulting from the intake of mineral oil is that it

    A. adds calories
    B. reduces weight
    C. impairs the appetite
    D. dissolves vitamin A

17. The leavening power of baking powders results from chemical action which releases

    A. carbon monoxide
    B. carbon dioxide
    C. cream of tartar
    D. lactic acid

18. The diet prescribed in diverticulitis is one that is

    A. high in calorie value
    B. high in roughage content
    C. low residue, bland
    D. high protein, bland

19. In typhoid fever, the diet should be

    A. *high* in calories and residue
    B. *low* in calories, high in residue
    C. *high* in calories, low in residue
    D. *high* in fruit juice content

20. Allspice is derived from

    A. the berry of the pimento tree
    B. a mixture of nutmeg, cinnamon and cloves
    C. the root of the allspice tree
    D. the bark of the cassia tree

21. Among the following food additives, the one which is used for the purpose of enhancing the keeping quality of the food is

    A. vitamin D in milk
    B. bleaching agents in flour
    C. ascorbic acid in cider
    D. minerals and vitamins in cereals

22. An example of the bactericidal method of food preservation is

    A. jam and jellies
    B. pickling
    C. freezing
    D. refrigeration

23. The material which destroys the activity of biotin is

    A. the protein found in uncooked egg white
    B. fluorides in drinking water
    C. iodides in medications
    D. fluorescent substances found in milk

24. Egg whites beat BEST if they are

    A. warm
    B. chilled thoroughly
    C. at room temperature
    D. beaten by hand

25. The RICHEST food sources of folacin are

    A. livers and green leafy vegetables
    B. eggs and milk
    C. cereals
    D. fats

KEY (CORRECT ANSWERS)

1. D
2. D
3. B
4. A
5. C

6. A
7. C
8. C
9. C
10. A

11. A
12. C
13. A
14. D
15. D

16. D
17. B
18. C
19. C
20. A

21. C
22. A
23. A
24. C
25. A

TEST 2

DIRECTIONS: Each question or incomplete statement is followed by several suggested answers or completions. Select the one that BEST answers the question or completes the statement. *PRINT THE LETTER OF THE CORRECT ANSWER IN THE SPACE AT THE RIGHT.*

1. Riboflavin is easily destroyed by 1.____
   - A. alkalies and light
   - B. acids and oxygen
   - C. heat and agitation
   - D. air and agitation

2. Cretinism is a form of idiocy due to extreme deficiency of secretion by 2.____
   - A. fat-soluble vitamins in the diet
   - B. B-complex vitamins in the diet
   - C. thyroid gland
   - D. adrenal glands

3. Nyctalopia results from a lack of 3.____
   - A. vitamin A
   - B. fluorine
   - C. citric acid
   - D. flavinoids

4. The MAJOR influence in the decline of endemic goiter in the United States is the use of 4.____
   - A. saffron oil
   - B. homogenized milk
   - C. iodized salt
   - D. enriched cereals

5. The Food Drug & Cosmetic Act of 1934 provides for 5.____
   - A. retention of nutritive values
   - B. fair pricing of goods
   - C. purity of content
   - D. accurate labeling

6. The liver is the storage depot in the body for vitamin 6.____
   - A. A
   - B. E
   - C. C
   - D. B

7. The anti-xerophthalmia vitamin is vitamin 7.____
   - A. A
   - B. B
   - C. E
   - D. K

8. The pathway of excretion of the nitrogenous end products of protein metabolism is the 8.____
   - A. lungs
   - B. skin
   - C. kidneys
   - D. large intestine

9. The term *trace elements* refers to 9.____
   - A. minerals needed in very small amounts in nutrition
   - B. substances which trace circulation in the body
   - C. tools used in sewing
   - D. potent drugs used as pain killer

10. Flavinoids which are effective in human health are

    A. biotics
    B. bioflavinoids
    C. neoflavinoids
    D. vitamins

11. Uric acid results from

    A. vitamin deficiency
    B. metabolism of purines
    C. digestion of carbohydrates
    D. injection of nicotine

12. Studies comparing the desirability of feeding to premature infants formulas warmed to body temperature and those given directly on removal from the refrigerator show

    A. no significant difference
    B. disturbed sleep following intake of cold formula
    C. regurgitation following intake of cold formula
    D. slower weight gain with cold feeding

13. Hypoglycemia is a condition of

    A. diseased eyes
    B. B, low blood sugar
    C. high blood sugar
    D. low purin content

14. The normal source of insulin in the human body is the

    A. liver
    B. thymus
    C. pancreas
    D. pineal gland

15. One of the earliest symptoms of a thiamine deficiency is

    A. polyneuritis
    B. anorexia
    C. nyctalopia
    D. conjunctivitis

16. Air is used as a leavening agent in

    A. sponge cake
    B. pound cake
    C. cookies
    D. bread

17. Cheese originates in

    A. pasteurization
    B. fermentation
    C. inversion
    D. coagulation

18. In measuring vitamin A value in foods, the International Unit is defined as the activity of

    A. 5.0 mg. calciferol
    B. 6.0 gm. tocopherol
    C. 6.0 gm. carotene
    D. 0.6 meg. betacarotene

19. In the last fifty years, the proportion of calories from milk, cheese, fruits, and vegetables in the American diet has

    A. remained the same
    B. doubled
    C. tripled
    D. quadrupled

20. Interference with absorption of vitamin A may result from

    A. a diet heavy with bulk foods
    B. overconsumption of salad oils
    C. mineral oil in salad dressings
    D. low cholesterol diet

20.____

21. Vitamin A food value is

    A. lacking in yams
    B. fairly constant in dairy products
    C. closely related to green coloring in vegetables
    D. closely related to sun available during growing time

21.____

22. The passage of digested substances into the villi for distribution through the body is called

    A. absorption   B. metabolism
    C. anabolism   D. peristalsis

22.____

23. Of the following, the RICHEST source of vitamin E is

    A. liver   B. green leafy vegetables
    C. wheat germ oil   D. egg yolk

23.____

24. Of the following, the number of calories which MOST NEARLY approximates the daily fuel needs of a moderately active 25-year-old woman is

    A. 1500   B. 2000   C. 2500   D. 3500

24.____

25. A deficiency of riboflavin results in

    A. xerophthalmia   B. polyneuritis
    C. cutaneous lesions   D. chielosis

25.____

KEY (CORRECT ANSWERS)

1.	A	11.	B
2.	C	12.	A
3.	A	13.	B
4.	C	14.	C
5.	D	15.	B
6.	A	16.	A
7.	A	17.	B
8.	C	18.	D
9.	A	19.	B
10.	B	20.	C

21. C
22. A
23. C
24. C
25. B

———

EXAMINATION SECTION
TEST 1

DIRECTIONS: Each question or incomplete statement is followed by several suggested answers or completions. Select the one that BEST answers the question or completes the statement. *PRINT THE LETTER OF THE CORRECT ANSWER IN THE SPACE AT THE RIGHT.*

1. The B vitamin folate may help prevent all of the following EXCEPT

    A. heart disease
    B. stroke
    C. prostate cancer
    D. colon cancer
    E. birth defects

    1.____

2. If you are older than 55, which is the best source of vitamin B_{12}?

    A. Milk
    B. Poultry
    C. Eggs
    D. Green leafy vegetables
    E. A vitamin supplement

    2.____

3. All of the following EXCEPT _____ can be a sign of vitamin B_{12} deficiency.

    A. memory loss
    B. excessive thirst
    C. mental confusion
    D. blurred vision
    E. tingling in the feet

    3.____

4. Which B vitamin can cause nerve damage if taken in high doses?

    A. Thiamin (B_1)
    B. Riboflavin (B_2)
    C. Niacin (B_3)
    D. Pyridoxine (B_6)

    4.____

5. All of the following EXCEPT _____ may lower the risk of heart disease.

    A. vitamin B_2
    B. vitamin B_6
    C. vitamin E
    D. folate
    E. fiber-rich foods

    5.____

6. Getting enough calcium may help cut the risk of _____ cancer.

    A. breast   B. bladder   C. colon   D. prostate

    6.____

7. People over age 50 should get 1,200 mg of calcium a day. That's the amount in all of the following EXCEPT

    A. four cups of milk
    B. six ounces of cheddar cheese
    C. nine cups of cottage cheese
    D. five cups of cooked broccoli
    E. four cups of calcium-fortified orange juice

    7.____

8. What is the maximum daily dose of calcium that is considered safe?

    A. 1,500 mg   B. 2,500 mg   C. 3,500 mg
    D. 4,500 mg   E. no limit

    8.____

9. Vitamin D may help prevent or treat all of the following EXCEPT

   A. high blood pressure
   B. hip fractures
   C. osteoarthritis
   D. osteoporosis

10. If you are middle-aged, all of the following EXCEPT _____ can supply a day's worth of vitamin D.

    A. a multivitamin
    B. a highly fortified cereal like Product 19 or Total
    C. four glasses of milk
    D. exposing your hands, face, and arms to the sun for five to ten minutes two or three times a week in the summer months (anywhere) or at any time of the year (in the South)

11. All of the following EXCEPT _____ helps to prevent high blood pressure.

    A. limiting sodium (salt)
    B. consuming enough potassium
    C. getting enough vitamin E
    D. eating enough fruits and vegetables
    E. getting enough exercise

12. All of the following EXCEPT _____ are good sources of potassium.

    A. bananas
    B. milk
    C. dry beans
    D. rye bread
    E. chicken

13. Too much iron can raise the risk of all of the following EXCEPT

    A. memory loss
    B. heart disease
    C. cancer
    D. liver damage

14. Evidence suggests that all of the following EXCEPT _____ lowers your risk of diabetes.

    A. staying lean
    B. eating fiber-rich foods
    C. eating enough magnesium
    D. eating enough potassium
    E. getting enough exercise

15. Evidence indicates that all of the following EXCEPT _____ may cut the risk of prostate cancer.

    A. magnesium
    B. lycopene
    C. selenium
    D. vitamin E
    E. eating less meat

16. Which is the best source of vitamin E?

    A. Whole-wheat bread
    B. Olive oil
    C. Broccoli
    D. Almonds
    E. Beans

17. Which can impair the immune system if taken in large doses?

    A. Copper
    B. Iron
    C. Zinc
    D. Vitamin A

18. According to the latest estimates, how much vitamin C do most people need each day? _____ mg.

    A. 60 B. 200 C. 500 D. 1,000 E. 5,000

19. All of the following EXCEPT _____ appears to help strengthen bones.

    A. vitamin D B. vitamin K
    C. vitamin E D. fluoride

20. A deficiency of _____ cannot be detected by a blood test.

    A. vitamin B_{12} B. vitamin D
    C. zinc D. iron

21. Which is the best source of selenium?

    A. Whole-wheat bread
    B. Spinach
    C. Fortified breakfast cereal
    D. A supplement

22. High doses of vitamin A or its precursor (betacarotene) may raise the risk of all of the following EXCEPT

    A. colon cancer B. lung cancer
    C. liver damage D. birth defects

23. Which one of the following appears to curb the muscle damage caused by exercise in people older than 55?

    A. Vitamin A B. Vitamin B_1
    C. Vitamin C D. Vitamin E

24. All of the following EXCEPT _____ are good sources of magnesium.

    A. bran cereal B. cantaloupe C. spinach
    D. black beans E. yogurt

25. Which food may protect your eyes as you age?

    A. Collard greens B. Soybeans
    C. Purple grape juice D. Carrots

26. Which supplement is MOST likely to do what its proponents claim it does?

    A. Echinacea B. Lecithin
    C. Saw palmetto D. DHEA

27. Which supplement is LEAST likely to do what its proponents claim it does?

    A. Glucosamine B. St. John's wort
    C. Kava kava D. Ginseng

28. All of the following EXCEPT _____ are rich sources of omega-3 fats.

    A. cod B. sardines
    C. rainbow trout D. salmon

29. Adverse effects of contaminants have been reported for all of the following EXCEPT

    A. ephedra
    B. DHEA
    C. 5-HTP
    D. chondroitin

30. Which one of the following is MOST likely to improve your memory?

    A. Vitamin E
    B. Phosphatidyl serine
    C. Lecithin
    D. Ginkgo biloba

5 (#1)

KEY (CORRECT ANSWERS)

1. CORRECT ANSWER: C
   Women who could become pregnant should take a multivitamin with 400 mcg, the Daily Value for folate. That amount helps prevent neural tube birth defects. Though more studies are needed, the same level also appears to cut the risk of heart disease, stroke, and colon cancer.

2. CORRECT ANSWER: E
   In younger people, all but the vegetables would be a good source of B_{12} (which is only found in animal foods). But if you are over 55, your stomach might not produce enough acid to extract the B_{12} from food. To play it safe, take a daily dose of 25 mcg, the amount in many supplements for seniors.

3. CORRECT ANSWER: B
   Vitamin B_{12} deficiency can cause irreversible nerve damage. If you have any of the symptoms (other than excessive thirst), get your B_{12} blood levels checked. Anemia can also be a sign of B_{12} deficiency, but you can get nerve damage without anemia. (Excessive thirst could be a sign of diabetes.)

4. CORRECT ANSWER: D
   The B-vitamins — like other water-soluble nutrients — are usually safe at high doses. B_6 is the exception. The Tolerable Upper Intake Level (UL) was set at 100 mg because higher daily doses can cause a (reversible) nerve toxicity that leads to difficulty walking, clumsiness, numbness, or burning, shooting, or tingling pains. The Daily Value for B_6 is only 2 mg.

5. CORRECT ANSWER: A
   People who consume more vitamin B_6 (about 4.6 mg a day), folate (at least 400 mcg a day), or vitamin E (at least 100 IU a day) have a lower risk of heart attacks. Vitamin B_6 and folate may protect the heart by lowering blood levels of homocysteine. None of the research is definitive, though. Clear answers about vitamin E may come from clinical trials that are under way to see if it can prevent heart attacks.

6. CORRECT ANSWER: C
   In a study of people who already had precancerous colon polyps, taking 1,200 mg of calcium a day cut the risk of new polyps by 24 percent. However, preliminary evidence suggests that men who consumed 2,000 mg of calcium a day — from food or supplements — had a higher risk of prostate cancer than men who consumed lower levels. Until we know more, men should not assume that more calcium is better.

7. CORRECT ANSWER: D
   Each cup of cooked broccoli has 70 mg of calcium, so you would need 17 cups to get a day's worth of calcium (not that you need to get all your calcium from a single food). Collards (with 230 mg per cup) and cooked frozen kale (with 180 mg per cup) are richer sources.

8. **CORRECT ANSWER: B**
   In 1997, the National Academy of Sciences set an Upper Tolerable Intake Level (UL) for calcium of 2,500 mg a day. Too much calcium can cause kidney stones, high blood calcium, or impaired absorption of iron, zinc, or magnesium. But 2,500 mg a day is not a target. Shoot for 2,000 mg a day if you are 19 to 50 and 1,200 mg a day if you are older than 50.

9. **CORRECT ANSWER: A**
   In a recent study in Boston, half of the women with hip fractures were deficient in vitamin D. So far, only one study has found slower progression of arthritis in people with low D levels.

10. **CORRECT ANSWER: B**
    Milk – not other dairy products – is one of the few good sources of vitamin D. Even cereals with 100 percent of the Daily Value for other vitamins and minerals do not supply much D. Experts recommend 200 IU a day if you are 19 to 50, 400 IU a day if you are 51 to 70, and 600 IU a day if you are older than 70. As people age, their skin gets less efficient at making vitamin D when exposed to the sun. You cannot get enough vitamin D from the sun in the winter unless you live in the Southern United States.

11. **CORRECT ANSWER: C**
    Avoiding overweight and limiting alcohol (to no more than one drink a day for women; two for men) also keep blood pressure from rising.

12. **CORRECT ANSWER: D**
    Fruits and vegetables, especially beans (except green beans), are the best sources. Whole grains have more than their refined cousins (almost all rye breads are refined), but even whole-wheat bread isn't loaded with potassium. Bran cereals are a better source. Most multivitamin-and-mineral supplements and fortified breakfast cereals don't supply much potassium.

13. **CORRECT ANSWER: A**
    Too little iron can impair memory and learning in adolescent girls (iron deficiency is less common in boys). But too much may raise the risk of cancer and heart disease. About one in 250 Americans has the genes for iron overload, or hemochromato-sis, which can damage the liver, heart, brain, pancreas, and other organs. To play it safe, get your blood ferritin checked. If you're male or postmenopausal, look for a multivitamin that supplies no more than 10 mg of iron a day. The 18 mg in most multis is the recommended allowance for teenage boys.

14. **CORRECT ANSWER: D**
    It's clear that extra pounds raise the risk of diabetes. Exercise lowers the risk, even if you're not overweight. The evidence for fiber-rich foods and magnesium, while promising, is shakier.

15. **CORRECT ANSWER: A**
    In separate clinical trials, men who took 200 mcg of selenium or 50 IU of vitamin E every day had a lower risk of prostate cancer. Studies are under way to duplicate those results. There are no trials on lycopene or red meat. However, men who eat less red meat – and less animal fat – seem to have a lower risk. Ditto for men who have higher blood levels of lycopene or who eat more lycopene-rich tomato-containing foods, especially cooked foods like tomato sauce.

16. CORRECT ANSWER: D
Almonds are the best of the bunch, with 11 IU in three tablespoons. But only supplements have the amounts that may help reduce the risk of heart disease (100 IU a day) or prostate cancer (50 IU a day).

17. CORRECT ANSWER: C
Zinc can impair the immune system at daily doses as low as 50 mg (in addition to the 15 mg in a typical diet). Vitamin A can cause liver damage and possibly birth defects at daily doses of 10,000 IU or more. Vitamin B_6 can cause (reversible) nerve damage at doses of 200 mg or more

18. CORRECT ANSWER: B
The current Daily Value is 60 mg, but some vitamin C experts think that intakes should be at least 100 mg or, more likely, 200 mg. If you eat the eight to ten servings of fruits and vegetables a day that we recommend, you should get at least 200 mg. So far there is no Upper Tolerable Level (UL) for vitamin C. It should be 1,000 mg a day, some argue, because more than that may raise the risk of kidney stones.

19. CORRECT ANSWER: C
Most people know that calcium and vitamin D are crucial for strong bones. But it's also important to get enough vitamin K. Women should shoot for 65 mcg a day, while men need 80 mcg. Green leafy vegetables are the best source. Most people get sufficient fluoride from fluoridated water.

20. CORRECT ANSWER: C
There is no good way to test for zinc deficiency. Instead, researchers give people more zinc and see if it improves the symptoms of a deficiency – diminished taste, wounds that take long to heal, or recurring infections that don't clear up easily. As for the other nutrients, it's worth getting your blood tested for 25-hydroxyvitamin D, serum ferritin (to see if you get too little or too much iron), and vitamin B_{12}.

21. CORRECT ANSWER: D
Seafood is the most reliable food source of selenium. The selenium content of other foods varies depending on where they were grown. If you want to get 200 mcg a day the amount that may cut the risk of cancer the safest way is to take a supplement.

22. CORRECT ANSWER: A
As little as 10,000 IU a day of vitamin A may raise the risk of birth defects when taken by pregnant women and may cause liver damage when taken by older people for 10 to 15 years. Beta-carotene doesn't cause birth defects or liver damage, but two studies found an increased risk of lung cancer in smokers who took 33,000 IU to 50,000 IU (20 mg to 30 mg) of beta-carotene a day for several years. In contrast, beta-carotene-rich foods, like carrots, sweet potatoes, and cantaloupe, are linked to a lower risk of lung cancer.

23. CORRECT ANSWER: D
When sedentary older people were told to exercise for 45 minutes a day, those who were given vitamin E had fewer signs of muscle damage than those who took a placebo. The study used 800 IU a day, but as little as 200 IU to 400 IU may be sufficient.

24. CORRECT ANSWER: B
Most fruits are not especially rich in magnesium. Nor are most vegetables, except for leafy greens and dry beans. Whole (not refined) grains and milk or yogurt can help you reach 320 mg (women) or 420 mg (men) a day. Most multivitamin-and-mineral supplements and fortified breakfast cereals supply only about 100 mg per serving.

25. CORRECT ANSWER: A
Studies suggest that foods rich in lutein, a carotenoid found in green leafy vegetables, may help prevent macular degeneration, the most common cause of blindness in older people. (The macula is the center of the retina.)

26. CORRECT ANSWER: C
There is consistent evidence that a daily dose of 320 mg of saw palmetto can help men with benign prostatic hypertrophy (enlarged prostates). The evidence for the others is inconclusive.

27. CORRECT ANSWER: D
Glucosamine seems to curb arthritis pain, St. John's wort appears to help one out of two people with clinical depression (whether it *cures the blues* for people who aren't clinically depressed is untested), and kava kava may help people with clinical anxiety (it's less certain whether it *relieves daily stress* or helps you relax). So far, there is insufficient evidence that ginseng is good for memory, energy, sexual interest or potency, symptoms of menopause, or the immune system.

28. CORRECT ANSWER: A
In some studies, people who consumed about 1.5 grams of omega-3 fats a week had a lower risk of heart attacks. You can get that much in six ounces of cooked (eight ounces of raw) salmon or rainbow trout or three ounces of canned sardines. A six-ounce serving of most other fish, including cod, flounder, tuna, clans, catfish, haddock, perch, and halibut, has between 0.2 and 0.9 grams of omega-3 fats.

29. CORRECT ANSWER: D
Experts are concerned that DHEA may raise testosterone levels, which may increase the risk of prostate cancer. Ephedra has been linked to about three dozen deaths and more than a thousand adverse reactions. And a half dozen samples of 5-HTP tested by the FDA contained a contaminant like the one that caused eosino-philia myalgia — a painful and sometimes disabling muscle disorder — in people who took trytophan supplements in the late 1980's.

30. CORRECT ANSWER: B
So far, the evidence is strongest that phosphatidyl serine (PS) can boost memory in healthy people with greater-than-normal age-related losses.

EXAMINATION SECTION
TEST 1

DIRECTIONS: Each question or incomplete statement is followed by several suggested answers or completions. Select the one that BEST answers the question or completes the statement. *PRINT THE LETTER OF THE CORRECT ANSWER IN THE SPACE AT THE RIGHT.*

1. When conducting a needs assessment for the purpose of education planning, an agency's FIRST step is to identify or provide
   A. a profile of population characteristics
   B. barriers to participation
   C. existing resources
   D. profiles of competing resources

   1.____

2. Research has demonstrated that of the following, the MOST effective medium for communicating with external publics is(are)
   A. video news releases
   B. television
   C. radio
   D. newspapers

   2.____

3. Basic ideas behind the effort to influence the attitudes and behaviors of a constituency include each of the following EXCEPT the idea that
   A. words, rather than actions or events, are most likely to motivate
   B. demands for action are a usual response
   C. self-interest usually figures heavily into public involvement
   D. the reliability of change programs is difficult to assess

   3.____

4. An agency representative is trying to craft a pithy message to constituents in order to encourage the use of agency program resources.
   Choosing an audience for such messages is easiest when the message
   A. is project- or behavior-based
   B. is combined with other messages
   C. is abstract
   D. has a broad appeal

   4.____

5. Of the following factors, the MOST important to the success of an agency's external education or communication programs is the
   A. amount of resources used to implement them
   B. public's prior experiences with the agency
   C. real value of the program to the public
   D. commitment of the internal audience

   5.____

6. A representative for a state agency is being interviewed by a reporter from a local news network. The representative is being asked to defend a program that is extremely unpopular in certain parts of the municipality.
   When a constituency is known to be opposed to a position, the MOST useful communication strategy is to present

   6.____

A. only the arguments that are consistent with constituents' views
B. only the agency's side of the issue
C. both sides of the argument as clearly as possible
D. both sides of the argument, omitting key information about the opposing position

7. The MOST significant barriers to effective agency community relations include
   I. widespread distrust of communication strategies
   II. the media's "watchdog" stance
   III. public apathy
   IV. statutory opposition

   The CORRECT answer is:
   A. I only   B. I and II   C. II and III   D. III and IV

8. In conducting an education program, many agencies use workshops and seminars in a classroom setting.
   Advantages of classroom-style teaching over other means of educating the public include each of the following, EXCEPT
   A. enabling an instructor to verify learning through testing and interaction with the target audience
   B. enabling hands-on practice and other participatory learning techniques
   C. ability to reach an unlimited number of participants in a given length of time
   D. ability to convey the latest, most up-to-date information

9. The _____ model of community relations is characterized by an attempt to persuade the public to adopt the agency's point of view.
   A. two-way symmetric   B. two-way asymmetric
   C. public information   D. press agency/publicity

10. Important elements of an internal situation analysis include the
    I. list of agency opponents   II. communication audit
    III. updated organizational almanac IV. stakeholder analysis

    The CORRECT answer is:
    A. I and II   B. I, II, and III   C. II and III   D. I, II, III and IV

11. Government agency information efforts typically involve each of the following objectives, EXCEPT to
    A. implement changes in the policies of government agencies to align with public opinion
    B. communicate the work of agencies
    C. explain agency techniques in a way that invites input from citizens
    D. provide citizen feedback to government administrators

12. Factors that are likely to influence the effectiveness of an educational campaign include the
   I. level of homogeneity among intended participants
   II. number and types of media used
   III. receptivity of the intended participants
   IV. level of specificity in the message or behavior to be taught

   The CORRECT answer is:
   A. I and II   B. I, II, and III   C. II and III   D. I, II, III, and IV

13. An agency representative is writing instructional objectives that will later help to measure the effectiveness of an educational program.
   Which of the following verbs, included in an objective, would be MOST helpful for the purpose of measuring effectiveness?
   A. Know   B. Identify   C. Learn   D. Comprehend

14. A state education agency wants to encourage participation in a program that has just received a boost through new federal legislation. The program is intended to include participants from a wide variety of socioeconomic and other demographic characteristics. The agency wants to launch a broad-based program that will inform virtually every interested party in the state about the program's new circumstances.
   In attempting to deliver this message to such a wide-ranging constituency, the agency's BEST practice would be to
   A. broadcast the same message through as many different media channels as possible
   B. focus on one discrete segment of the public at a time
   C. craft a message whose appeal is as broad as the public itself
   D. let the program's achievements speak for themselves and rely on word-of-mouth

15. Advantages associated with using the World Wide Web as an educational tool include
   I. an appeal to younger generations of the public
   II. visually-oriented, interactive learning
   III. learning that is not confined by space, time, or institutional association
   IV. a variety of methods for verifying use and learning

   The CORRECT answer is:
   A. I only   B. I and II   C. I, II, and III   D. I, II, II, and IV

16. In agencies involved in health care, community relations is a critical function because it
   A. serves as an intermediary between the agency and consumers
   B. generates a clear mission statement for agency goals and priorities
   C. ensures patient privacy while satisfying the media's right to information
   D. helps marketing professionals determine the wants and needs of agency constituents

17. After an extensive campaign to promote its newest program to constituents, an agency learns that most of the audience did not understand the intended message.
MOST likely, the agency has
    A. chosen words that were intended to inform, rather than persuade
    B. not accurately interpreted what the audience really needed to know
    C. overestimated the ability of the audience to receive and process the message
    D. compensated for noise that may have interrupted the message

18. The necessary elements that lead to conviction and motivation in the minds of participants in an educational or information program include each of the following, EXCEPT the _____ of the message.
    A. acceptability
    B. intensity
    C. single-channel appeal
    D. pervasiveness

19. Printed materials are often at the core of educational programs provided by public agencies.
The PRIMARY disadvantage associated with print is that it
    A. does not enable comprehensive treatment of a topic
    B. is generally unreliable in term of assessing results
    C. is often the most expensive medium available
    D. is constrained by time

20. Traditional thinking on public opinion holds that there is about _____ percent of the public who are pivotal to shifting the balance and momentum of opinion—they are concerned about an issue, but not fanatical, and interested enough to pay attention to a reasoned discussion.
    A. 2
    B. 10
    C. 33
    D. 51

21. One of the most useful guidelines for influencing attitude change among people is to
    A. invite the target audience to come to you, rather than approaching them
    B. use moral appeals as the primary approach
    C. use concrete images to enable people to see the results of behaviors or indifference
    D. offer tangible rewards to people for changes in behavior

22. An agency is attempting to evaluate the effectiveness of its educational program. For this purpose, it wants to observe several focus groups discussing the same program.
Which of the following would NOT be a guideline for the use of focus groups?
    A. Focus groups should only include those who have participated in the program.
    B. Be sure to accurately record the discussion.
    C. The same questions should be asked at each focus group meeting.
    D. It is often helpful to have a neutral, non-agency employee facilitate discussions.

23. Research consistently shows that _____ is the determinant most likely to make a newspaper editor run a news release.
    A. novelty   B. prominence   C. proximity   D. conflict

24. Which of the following is NOT one of the major variables to take into account when considering a population-needs assessment?
    A. State of program development   B. Resources available
    C. Demographics   D. Community attitudes

25. The FIRST step in any communications audit is to
    A. develop a research instrument
    B. determine how the organization currently communicates
    C. hire a contractor
    D. determine which audience to assess

KEY (CORRECT ANSWERS)

1. A		11. A	
2. D		12. D	
3. A		13. B	
4. A		14. B	
5. D		15. C	
6. C		16. A	
7. D		17. B	
8. C		18. C	
9. B		19. B	
10. C		20. B	

21. C
22. A
23. C
24. C
25. D

TEST 2

DIRECTIONS: Each question or incomplete statement is followed by several suggested answers or completions. Select the one that BEST answers the question or completes the statement. *PRINT THE LETTER OF THE CORRECT ANSWER IN THE SPACE AT THE RIGHT.*

1. A public relations practitioner at an agency has just composed a press release highlighting a program's recent accomplishments and success stories.
   In pitching such releases to print outlets, the practitioner should
   I. e-mail, mail, or send them by messenger
   II. address them to "editor" or "news director"
   III. have an assistant call all media contacts by telephone
   IV. ask reporters or editors how they prefer to receive them

   The CORRECT answer is:
   A. I and II B. I and IV C. II, III, and IV D. III only   1._____

2. The "output goals" of an educational program are MOST likely to include   2._____
   A. specified ratings of services by participants on a standardized scale
   B. observable effects on a given community or clientele
   C. the number of instructional hours provided
   D. the number of participants served

3. An agency wants to evaluate satisfaction levels among program participants, and mails out questionnaires to everyone who has been enrolled in the last year.
   The PRIMARY problem associated with this method of evaluative research is that it   3._____
   A. poses a significant inconvenience for respondents
   B. is inordinately expensive
   C. does not allow for follow-up or clarification questions
   D. usually involves a low response rate

4. A communications audit is an important tool for measuring   4._____
   A. the depth of penetration of a particular message or program
   B. the cost of the organization's information campaigns
   C. how key audiences perceive an organization
   D. the commitment of internal stakeholders

5. The "ABCs" of written learning objectives include each of the following, EXCEPT   5._____
   A. Audience   B. Behavior   C. Conditions   D. Delineation

23. Research consistently shows that _____ is the determinant most likely to make a newspaper editor run a news release.
    A. novelty   B. prominence   C. proximity   D. conflict

24. Which of the following is NOT one of the major variables to take into account when considering a population-needs assessment?
    A. State of program development   B. Resources available
    C. Demographics   D. Community attitudes

25. The FIRST step in any communications audit is to
    A. develop a research instrument
    B. determine how the organization currently communicates
    C. hire a contractor
    D. determine which audience to assess

KEY (CORRECT ANSWERS)

1.	A		11.	A
2.	D		12.	D
3.	A		13.	B
4.	A		14.	B
5.	D		15.	C
6.	C		16.	A
7.	D		17.	B
8.	C		18.	C
9.	B		19.	B
10.	C		20.	B

21. C
22. A
23. C
24. C
25. D

TEST 2

DIRECTIONS: Each question or incomplete statement is followed by several suggested answers or completions. Select the one that BEST answers the question or completes the statement. *PRINT THE LETTER OF THE CORRECT ANSWER IN THE SPACE AT THE RIGHT.*

1. A public relations practitioner at an agency has just composed a press release highlighting a program's recent accomplishments and success stories.
   In pitching such releases to print outlets, the practitioner should
   I. e-mail, mail, or send them by messenger
   II. address them to "editor" or "news director"
   III. have an assistant call all media contacts by telephone
   IV. ask reporters or editors how they prefer to receive them

   The CORRECT answer is:
   A. I and II B. I and IV C. II, III, and IV D. III only

   1._____

2. The "output goals" of an educational program are MOST likely to include
   A. specified ratings of services by participants on a standardized scale
   B. observable effects on a given community or clientele
   C. the number of instructional hours provided
   D. the number of participants served

   2._____

3. An agency wants to evaluate satisfaction levels among program participants, and mails out questionnaires to everyone who has been enrolled in the last year.
   The PRIMARY problem associated with this method of evaluative research is that it
   A. poses a significant inconvenience for respondents
   B. is inordinately expensive
   C. does not allow for follow-up or clarification questions
   D. usually involves a low response rate

   3._____

4. A communications audit is an important tool for measuring
   A. the depth of penetration of a particular message or program
   B. the cost of the organization's information campaigns
   C. how key audiences perceive an organization
   D. the commitment of internal stakeholders

   4._____

5. The "ABCs" of written learning objectives include each of the following, EXCEPT
   A. Audience B. Behavior C. Conditions D. Delineation

   5._____

6. When attempting to change the behaviors of constituents, it is important to keep in mind that
   I. most people are skeptical of communications that try to get them to change their behaviors
   II. in most cases, a person selects the media to which he exposes himself
   III. people tend to react defensively to messages or programs that rely on fear as a motivating factor
   IV. programs should aim for the broadest appeal possible in order to include as many participants as possible

   The CORRECT answer is:
   A. I and II   B. I, II and III   C. II and III   D. I, II, III, and IV

7. The "laws" of public opinion include the idea that it is
   A. useful for anticipating emergencies
   B. not sensitive to important events
   C. basically determined by self-interest
   D. sustainable through persistent appeals

8. Which of the following types of evaluations is used to measure public attitudes before and after an information/educational program?
   A. Retrieval study
   B. Copy test
   C. Quota sampling
   D. Benchmark study

9. The PRIMARY source for internal communications is(are) usually
   A. flow charts
   B. meetings
   C. voice mail
   D. printed publications

10. An agency representative is putting together informational materials—brochures and a newsletter—outlining changes in one of the state's biggest benefits programs.
    In assembling print materials as a medium for delivering information to the public, the representative should keep in mind each of the following trends:
    I. For various reasons, the reading capabilities of the public are in general decline
    II. Without tables and graphs to help illustrate the changes, it is unlikely that the message will be delivered effectively
    III. Professionals and career-oriented people are highly receptive to information written in the form of a journal article or empirical study
    IV. People tend to be put off by print materials that use itemized and bulleted (●) lists

    The CORRECT answer is:
    A. I and II   B. I, II and III   C. II and III   D. I, II, III, and IV

11. Which of the following steps in a problem-oriented information campaign would typically be implemented FIRST?
    A. Deciding on tactics
    B. Determining a communications strategy
    C. Evaluating the problem's impact
    D. Developing an organizational strategy

12. A common pitfall in conducting an educational program is to
    A. aim it at the wrong target audience
    B. overfund it
    C. leave it in the hands of people who are in the business of education, rather than those with expertise in the business of the organization
    D. ignore the possibility that some other organization is meeting the same educational need for the target audience

13. The key factors that affect the credibility of an agency's educational program include
    A. organization
    B. scope
    C. sophistication
    D. penetration

14. Research on public opinion consistently demonstrates that it is
    A. easy to move people toward a strong opinion on anything, as long as they are approached directly through their emotions
    B. easier to move people away from an opinion they currently hold than to have them form an opinion about something they have not previously cared about
    C. easy to move people toward a strong opinion on anything, as long as the message appeals to their reason and intellect
    D. difficult to move people toward a strong opinion on anything, no matter what the approach

15. In conducting an education program, many agencies use meetings and conferences to educate an audience about the organization and its programs. Advantages associated with this approach include
    I. a captive audience that is known to be interested in the topic
    II. ample opportunities for verifying learning
    III. cost-efficient meeting space
    IV. the ability to provide information on a wider variety of subjects

    The CORRECT answer is:
    A. I and II   B. I, III and IV   C. II and III   D. I, II, III and IV

16. An agency is attempting to evaluate the effectiveness of its educational programs. For this purpose, it wants to observe several focus groups discussing particular programs.
    For this purpose, a focus group should never number more than _____ participants.
    A. 5   B. 10   C. 15   D. 20

17. A _____ speech is written so that several agency members can deliver it to different audiences with only minor variations.
    A. basic   B. printed   C. quota   D. pattern

18. Which of the following statements about public opinion is generally considered to be FALSE?
    A. Opinion is primarily reactive rather than proactive.
    B. People have more opinions about goals than about the means by which to achieve them.
    C. Facts tend to shift opinion in the accepted direction when opinion is not solidly structured.
    D. Public opinion is based more on information than desire.

19. An agency is trying to promote its educational program.
    As a general rule, the agency should NOT assume that
    A. people will only participate if they perceive an individual benefit
    B. promotions need to be aimed at small, discrete groups
    C. if the program is good, the audience will find out about it
    D. a variety of methods, including advertising, special events, and direct mail, should be considered

20. In planning a successful educational program, probably the first and most important question for an agency to ask is:
    A. What will be the content of the program?
    B. Who will be served by the program?
    C. When is the best time to schedule the program?
    D. Why is the program necessary?

21. Media kits are LEAST likely to contain
    A. fact sheets   B. memoranda
    C. photographs with captions   D. news releases

22. The use of pamphlets and booklets as media for communication with the public often involves the disadvantage that
    A. the messages contained within them are frequently nonspecific
    B. it is difficult to measure their effectiveness in delivering the message
    C. there are few opportunities for people to refer to them
    D. color reproduction is poor

23. The MOST important prerequisite of a good educational program is an
    A. abundance of resources to implement it
    B. individual staff unit formed for the purpose of program delivery
    C. accurate needs assessment
    D. uneducated constituency

24. After an education program has been delivered, an agency conducts a program evaluation to determine whether its objectives have been met.
General rules about how to conduct such an education program valuation include each of the following, EXCEPT that it
   A. must be done immediately after the program has been implemented
   B. should be simple and easy to use
   C. should be designed so that tabulation of responses can take place quickly and inexpensively
   D. should solicit mostly subjective, open-ended responses if the audience was large

25. Using electronic media such as television as means of educating the public is typically recommended ONLY for agencies that
   I. have a fairly simple message to begin with
   II. want to reach the masses, rather than a targeted audience
   III. have substantial financial resources
   IV. accept that they will not be able to measure the results of the campaign with much precision

   The CORRECT answer is:
   A. I and II   B. I, II and III   C. II and IV   D. I, II, III and IV

KEY (CORRECT ANSWERS)

1.	B	11.	C
2.	C	12.	D
3.	D	13.	A
4.	C	14.	D
5.	D	15.	B
6.	B	16.	B
7.	C	17.	D
8.	D	18.	D
9.	D	19.	C
10.	A	20.	D

21.	B
22.	B
23.	C
24.	D
25.	D

PREPARING WRITTEN MATERIAL

PARAGRAPH REARRANGEMENT
COMMENTARY

The sentences that follow are in scrambled order. You are to rearrange them in proper order and indicate the letter choice containing the correct answer at the space at the right.

Each group of sentences in this section is actually a paragraph presented in scrambled order. Each sentence in the group has a place in that paragraph; no sentence is to be left out. You are to read each group of sentences and decide upon the best order in which to put the sentences so as to form a well-organized paragraph.

The questions in this section measure the ability to solve a problem when all the facts relevant to its solution are not given.

More specifically, certain positions of responsibility and authority require the employee to discover connection between events sometimes, apparently, unrelated. In order to do this, the employee will find it necessary to correctly infer that unspecified events have probably occurred or are likely to occur. This ability becomes especially important when action must be taken on incomplete information.

Accordingly, these questions require competitors to choose among several suggested alternatives, each of which presents a different sequential arrangement of the events. Competitors must choose the MOST logical of the suggested sequences.

In order to do so, they may be required to draw on general knowledge to infer missing concepts or events that are essential to sequencing the given events. Competitors should be careful to infer only what is essential to the sequence. The plausibility of the wrong alternatives will always require the inclusion of unlikely events or of additional chains of events which are NOT essential to sequencing the given events.

It's very important to remember that you are looking for the best of the four possible choices, and that the best choice of all may not even be one of the answers you're given to choose from.

There is no one right way to solve these problems. Many people have found it helpful to first write out the order of the sentences, as they would have arranged them, on their scrap paper before looking at the possible answers. If their optimum answer is there, this can save them some time. If it isn't, this method can still give insight into solving the problem. Others find it most helpful to just go through each of the possible choices, contrasting each as they go along. You should use whatever method feels comfortable and works for you.

While most of these types of questions are not that difficult, we've added a higher percentage of the difficult type, just to give you more practice. Usually there are only one or two questions on this section that contain such subtle distinctions that you're unable to answer confidently. And you then may find yourself stuck deciding between two possible choices, neither of which you're sure about.

EXAMINATION SECTION
TEST 1

DIRECTIONS: Each group of sentences in this section is actually a paragraph presented in scrambled order. Each sentence in the group has a place in that paragraph; no sentence is to be left out. You are to read each group of sentences, so as to form a well-organized paragraph. Before trying to answer the questions which follow each group of sentences, jot down the correct order of the sentences. Then answer each of the questions by printing the letter of the correct answer in the space at the right. Remember that you will receive credit only for answers marked.

P. The infant only feels the positive stimulation of warmth and food and does not differentiate the warmth and food from their source, mother.
Q. The infant, at the moment of birth, would feel the fear of dying if gracious fate did not preserve it from any awareness of the anxiety involved in the separation from mother.
R. The infant's state, then, is what has been called narcissism.
S. Mother is warmth, mother is food, mother is the euphoric state of satisfaction and security.
T. Even after being born, the infant is not yet aware of itself, and of the world as being outside of itself.

1. Which sentence did you put before Sentence Q?   1._____

   A. P
   B. R
   C. S
   D. T
   E. None of the above. Sentence Q is first.

2. Which sentence did you put after Sentence S?   2._____

   A. P
   B. Q
   C. R
   D. T
   E. None of the above. Sentence S is last.

3. Which sentence did you put before Sentence P?   3._____

   A. Q
   B. R
   C. S
   D. T
   E. None of the above. Sentence P is first.

2 (#1)

4. Which sentence did you put after Sentence P? 4.____

    A. Q
    B. R
    C. S
    D. T
    E. None of the above. Sentence P is last.

5. Which sentence did you put after Sentence R? 5.____

    A. P
    B. Q
    C. S
    D. T
    E. None of the above. Sentence R is last.

KEY (CORRECT ANSWERS)

1. E
2. C
3. D
4. C
5. E

TEST 2

DIRECTIONS: Each group of sentences in this section is actually a paragraph presented in scrambled order. Each sentence in the group has a place in that paragraph; no sentence is to be left out. You are to read each group of sentences, so as to form a well-organized paragraph. Before trying to answer the questions which follow each group of sentences, jot down the correct order of the sentences. Then answer each of the questions by printing the letter of the correct answer in the space at the right. Remember that you will receive credit only for answers marked.

P. Then it requires knowledge and effort.
Q. The former is my view.
R. Or is love a pleasant sensation, something one *falls into* if one is lucky?
S. The majority of people today, however, believe in the latter.
T. Is love an art?

1. Which sentence did you put second?
   A. P   B. Q   C. R   D. S   E. T

2. Which sentence did you put after Sentence S?
   A. P
   B. Q
   C. R
   D. T
   E. None of the above. Sentence S is last.

3. Which sentence did you put before Sentence Q?
   A. P
   B. R
   C. S
   D. T
   E. None of the above. Sentence Q is first.

4. Which sentence did you put before Sentence P?
   A. Q
   B. R
   C. S
   D. T
   E. None of the above. Sentence P is first.

5. Which sentence did you put after Sentence Q?
   A. P
   B. R
   C. S
   D. T
   E. None of the above. Sentence Q is last.

2 (#2)

KEY (CORRECT ANSWERS)

1. A
2. E
3. B
4. D
5. C

TEST 3

DIRECTIONS: Each group of sentences in this section is actually a paragraph presented in scrambled order. Each sentence in the group has a place in that paragraph; no sentence is to be left out. You are to read each group of sentences, so as to form a well-organized paragraph. Before trying to answer the questions which follow each group of sentences, jot down the correct order of the sentences. Then answer each of the questions by printing the letter of the correct answer in the space at the right. Remember that you will receive credit only for answers marked.

P. Indeed, in his time, Freud's theories of sex had a challenging and revolutionary character.
Q. Sexual mores have changed so much that Freud's theories no longer are shocking to the middle classes.
R. Freud has been criticized for his overevaluation of sex.
S. But what was true sixty years ago is no longer true.
T. This criticism resulted from a wish to remove an element from Freud's system which might arouse criticism among conventionally-minded people.

1. Which sentence did you put last?
   A. P   B. Q   C. R   D. S   E. T

2. Which sentence did you put before Sentence Q?
   A. P
   B. R
   C. S
   D. T
   E. None of the above. Sentence Q is first.

3. Which sentence did you put after Sentence T?
   A. P
   B. Q
   C. R
   D. S
   E. None of the above. Sentence T is last.

4. Which sentence did you put before Sentence R?
   A. P
   B. Q
   C. S
   D. T
   E. None of the above. Sentence R is first.

5. Which sentence did you put after Sentence R?
   A. P
   B. Q
   C. S
   D. T
   E. None of the above. Sentence R is last.

KEY (CORRECT ANSWERS)

1. B
2. C
3. A
4. E
5. D

TEST 4

DIRECTIONS: Each group of sentences in this section is actually a paragraph presented in scrambled order. Each sentence in the group has a place in that paragraph; no sentence is to be left out. You are to read each group of sentences, so as to form a well-organized paragraph. Before trying to answer the questions which follow each group of sentences, jot down the correct order of the sentences. Then answer each of the questions by printing the letter of the correct answer in the space at the right. Remember that you will receive credit only for answers marked.

P. Early Scandanavian accounts, as well, are too mythological and legendary to serve as history.
Q. The first trustworthy written evidence of a kingdom of Denmark belongs to the beginning of the Viking period.
R. Ancient Roman knowledge of this remote country was fragmentary and unreliable.
S. Archaeology and the study of place names, however, provide a certain amount of information about the earliest settlements.
T. Everything before that is prehistory.

1. Which sentence did you put fourth?
   A. P   B. B. Q   C. C. R   D. D. S   E. E. T

2. Which sentence did you put after Sentence T?
   A. Q
   B. R
   C. S
   D. None of the above. Sentence T is last.

3. Which sentence did you put after Sentence Q?
   A. P
   B. R
   C. S
   D. T
   E. None of the above. Sentence Q is last.

4. Which sentence did you put before Sentence Q?
   A. P
   B. R
   C. S
   D. T
   E. None of the above. Sentence Q is first.

5. Which sentence did you put after Sentence P?
   A. Q
   B. R
   C. S
   D. T
   E. None of the above. Sentence P is last.

KEY (CORRECT ANSWERS)

1. A
2. C
3. D
4. E
5. C

TEST 5

DIRECTIONS: Each group of sentences in this section is actually a paragraph presented in scrambled order. Each sentence in the group has a place in that paragraph; no sentence is to be left out. You are to read each group of sentences, so as to form a well-organized paragraph. Before trying to answer the questions which follow each group of sentences, jot down the correct order of the sentences. Then answer each of the questions by printing the letter of the correct answer in the space at the right. Remember that you will receive credit only for answers marked.

- P. In 1268, ambassadors were required to surrender all gifts they had received on their missions.
- Q. In the 13th century, the Venetian republic began to lay down rules of conduct for its ambassadors.
- R. In 1288, it was decreed that ambassadors were to report in writing on the results of their missions.
- S. Such reports are a mine of historical material.
- T. It is in Venice that the origins of modern diplomacy are to be sought.

1. Which sentence did you put second?
   A. P   B. Q   C. R   D. S   E. T

2. Which sentence did you put after Sentence R?
   A. P
   B. Q
   C. S
   D. T
   E. None of the above. Sentence R is last.

3. Which sentence did you put before Sentence P?
   A. Q
   B. R
   C. S
   D. T
   E. None of the above. Sentence P is first.

4. Which sentence did you put before Sentence T?
   A. P
   B. Q
   C. R
   D. S
   E. None of the above. Sentence T is first.

5. Which sentence did you put last?
   A. P   B. B. Q   C. C. R   D. D. S   E. E. T

KEY (CORRECT ANSWERS)

1. B
2. C
3. A
4. E
5. D

PREPARING WRITTEN MATERIALS
EXAMINATION SECTION
TEST 1

DIRECTIONS: Each question or incomplete statement is followed by several suggested answers or completions. Select the one that BEST answers the question or completes the statement. *PRINT THE LETTER OF THE CORRECT ANSWER IN THE SPACE AT THE RIGHT.*

Questions 1-21.

DIRECTIONS: In each of the following sentences, which were taken from students' transcripts, there may be an error. Indicate the appropriate correction in the space at the right. If the sentence is correct as is, indicate this choice. Unnecessary changes will be considered incorrect.

1. In that building there seemed to be representatives of Teachers College, the Veterans Bureau, and the Businessmen's Association.
   A. Teacher's College
   B. Veterans' Bureau
   C. Businessmens Association
   D. Correct as is

   1.____

2. In his travels, he visited St. Paul, San Francisco, Springfield, Ohio, and Washington, D.C.
   A. Ohio and
   B. Saint Paul
   C. Washington, D.C.
   D. Correct as is

   2.____

3. As a result of their purchasing a controlling interest in the syndicate, it was well-known that the Bureau of Labor Statistics' calculations would be unimportant.
   A. of them purchasing
   B. well known
   C. Statistics
   D. Correct as is

   3.____

4. Walter Scott, Jr.'s, attempt to emulate his father's success was doomed to failure.
   A. Junior's,
   B. Scott's, Jr.
   C. Scott, Jr.'s attempt
   D. Correct as is

   4.____

5. About B.C. 250 the Romans invaded Great Britain, and remains of their highly developed civilization can still be seen.
   A. 250 B.C.
   B. Britain and
   C. highly-developed
   D. Correct as is

   5.____

6. The two boss's sons visited the children's department.
   A. bosses   B. bosses'   C. childrens'   D. Correct as is

   6.____

121

7. Miss Amex not only approved the report, but also decided that it needed no revision.
   A. report; but
   B. report but
   C. report. But
   D. Correct as is

   7._____

8. Here's brain food in a jiffy—economical, too!
   A. economical too!
   B. "brain food"
   C. jiffy-economical
   D. Correct as is

   8._____

9. She said, "He likes the "Gatsby Look" very much."
   A. said "He
   B. "he
   C. 'Gatsby Look'
   D. Correct as is

   9._____

10. We anticipate that we will be able to visit them briefly in Los Angeles on Wednesday after a five day visit.
    A. Wednes-
    B. 5 day
    C. five-day
    D. Correct as is

    10._____

11. She passed all her tests, and, she now has a good position.
    A. tests, and she
    B. past
    C. tests;
    D. Correct as is

    11._____

12. The billing clerk said, "I will send the bill today"; however, that was a week ago, and it hasn't arrived yet!
    A. today;"
    B. today,"
    C. ago and
    D. Correct as is

    12._____

13. "She types at more-than-average speed," Miss Smith said, "but I feel that it is a result of marvelous concentration and self control on her part."
    A. more than average
    B. "But
    C. self-control
    D. Correct as is

    13._____

14. The state of Alaska, the largest state in the union, is also the northernmost state.
    A. Union
    B. Northernmost State
    C. State of Alaska
    D. Correct as is

    14._____

15. The memoirs of Ex-President Nixon, according to figures, sold more copies than Six Crises, the book he wrote in the '60s.
    A. Six Crises
    B. ex-President
    C. 60s
    D. Correct as is

    15._____

16. "There are three principal elements, determining the hazard of buildings: the contents hazard, the fire resistance of the structure, and the character of the interior finish," concluded the speaker.
    The one of the following statements that is MOST acceptable is that, in the above passage,
    A. the comma following the word *elements* is incorrect
    B. the colon following the word *buildings* is incorrect
    C. the comma following the word *finish* is incorrect
    D. there is no error in the punctuation of the sentence

    16._____

3 (#1)

17. He spoke on his favorite topic, "Why We Will Win." (How could I stop him?)   17.____
    A. Win".   B. him?).   C. him)?   C. Correct as is

18. "All any insurance policy is, is a contract for services," said my insurance   18.____
    agent, Mr. Newton.
    A. Insurance Policy   B. Insurance Agent
    C. policy is is a   D. Correct as is

19. Inasmuch as the price list has now been up dated, we should sent it to the   19.____
    printer.
    A. In as much   B. updated
    C. pricelist   D. Correct as is

20. We feel that "Our know-how" is responsible for the improvement in technical   20.____
    developments.
    A. "our   B. know how   C. that,   D. Correct as is

21. Did Cortez conquer the Incas? the Aztecs? the South American Indians?   21.____
    A. Incas, the Aztecs, the South American Indians?
    B. Incas; the Aztecs; the South American Indians?
    C. south American Indians?
    D. Correct as is

22. Which one of the following forms for the typed name of the dictator in the closing   22.____
    lines of a letter is generally MOST acceptable in the United States?
    A. (Dr.) James F. Farley   B. Dr. James F. Farley
    C. Me. James J. Farley, Ph.D.   D. James F. Farley

23. The plural of   23.____
    A. turkey is turkies   B. cargo is cargoes
    C. bankruptcy is bankruptcys   D. son-in-law is son-in-laws

24. The abbreviation viz. means MOST NEARLY   24.____
    A. namely   B. for example
    C. the following   D. see

25. In the sentence, *A man in a light-gray suit waited thirty-five minutes in the* 25.____
    ante-room for the all-important document, the word IMPROPERLY hyphenated
    is
    A. light-gray   B. thirty-five   C. ante-room   D. all-important

KEY (CORRECT ANSWERS)

1.	D		11.	A
2.	C		12.	D
3.	B		13.	D
4.	D		14.	A
5.	A		15.	B
6.	B		16.	A
7.	B		17.	D
8.	D		18.	D
9.	C		19.	B
10.	C		20.	A

21. D
22. D
23. B
24. A
25. C

TEST 2

DIRECTIONS: Each question or incomplete statement is followed by several suggested answers or completions. Select the one that BEST answers the question or completes the statement. *PRINT THE LETTER OF THE CORRECT ANSWER IN THE SPACE AT THE RIGHT.*

Questions 1-10.

DIRECTIONS: In each of the following groups of four sentences, one sentence contains an error in sentence structure, grammar, usage, diction, or punctuation. Indicate the INCORRECT sentence.

1. A. The lecture finished, the audience began asking questions.
   B. Any man who could accomplish that task the world would regard as a hero.
   C. Our respect and admiration are mutual.
   D. George did like his mother told him, despite the importunities of his playmates.

2. A. I cannot but help admiring you for your dedication to your job.
   B. Because they had insisted upon showing us films of their travels, we have lost many friends whom we once cherished.
   C. I am constrained to admit that your remarks made me feel bad.
   D. My brother having been notified of his acceptance by the university of his choice, my father immediately made plans for a vacation.

3. A. In no other country is freedom of speech and assembly so jealously guarded.
   B. Being a beatnik, he felt that it would be a betrayal of his cause to wear shoes and socks at the same time.
   C. Riding over the Brooklyn Bridge gave us an opportunity to see the Manhattan skyline.
   D. In 1961, flaunting SEATO, the North Vietnamese crossed the line of demarcation.

4. A. I have enjoyed the study of the Spanish language not only because of its beauty and the opportunity it offers to understand the Hispanic culture but also to make use of it in the business associations I have in South America.
   B. The opinions he expressed were decidedly different from those he had held in his youth.
   C. Had he actually studied, he certainly would have passed.
   D. A supervisor should be patient, tactful, and firm.

5. A. At this point we were faced with only three alternatives: to push on, to remain where we were, or to return to the village.
   B. We had no choice but to forgive so venial a sin.
   C. In their new picture, the Warners are flouting tradition.
   D. Photographs taken revealed that 2.5 square miles had been burned.

125

6. A. He asked whether he might write to his friends.
    B. There are many problems which must be solved before we can be assured of world peace.
    C. Each person with whom I talked expressed his opinion freely.
    D. Holding on to my saddle with all my strength the horse galloped down the road at a terrifying pace.

7. A. After graduating high school, he obtained a position as a runner in Wall Street.
    B. Last night, in a radio address, the President urged us to subscribe to the Red Cross.
    C. In the evening, light spring rain cooled the streets.
    D. "Un-American" is a word which has been used even by those whose sympathies may well have been pro-Nazi.

8. A. It is hard to conceive of their not doing good work.
    B. Who won—you or I?
    C. He having read the speech caused much comment.
    D. Their finishing the work proves that it can be done.

9. A. Our course of study should not be different now than it was five years ago.
    B. I cannot deny myself the pleasure of publicly thanking the mayor for his actions.
    C. The article on "Morale" has appeared in the Times Literary Supplement.
    D. He died of tuberculosis contracted during service with the Allied Forces.

10. A. If it wasn't for a lucky accident, he would still be an office-clerk.
    B. It is evident that teachers need help.
    C. Rolls of postage stamps may be bought at stationery stores.
    D. Addressing machines are used by firms that publish magazines.

11. The one of the following sentences which contains NO error in usage is:
    A. After the robbers left, the proprietor stood tied in his chair for about two hours before help arrived.
    B. In the cellar I found the watchmans' hat and coat.
    C. The persons living in adjacent apartments stated that they had heard no unusual noises.
    D. Neither a knife or any firearms were found in the room.

12. The one of the following sentences which contains NO error in usage is:
    A. The policeman lay a firm hand on the suspect's shoulder.
    B. It is true that neither strength nor agility are the most important requirement for a good patrolman.
    C. Good citizens constantly strive to do more than merely comply the restraints imposed by society.
    D. Twenty years is considered a severe sentence for a felony.

13. Select the sentence containing an adverbial objective. 13.____
    A. Concepts can only acquire content when they are connected, however indirectly, with sensible experience.
    B. The cloth was several shades too light to match the skirt which she had discarded.
    C. The Gargantuan Hall of Commons became a tri-daily horror to Kurt, because two youths discerned that he had a beard and courageously told the world about it.
    D. Brooding morbidly over the event, Elsie found herself incapable of engaging in normal activity.

14. Select the sentence containing a verb in the subjunctive mood. 14.____
    A. Had he known of the new experiments with penicillin dust for the cure of colds, he might have been tempted to try them in his own office.
    B. I should be very much honored by your visit.
    C. Though he has one of the highest intelligence quotients in his group, he seems far below the average in actual achievement.
    D. Long had I known that he would be the man finally selected for such signal honors.

15. Select the sentence containing one (or more) passive perfect participle(s). 15.____
    A. Having been apprised of the consequences of his refusal to answer, the witness finally revealed the source of his information.
    B. To have been placed in such an uncomfortable position was perhaps unfair to a journalist of his reputation.
    C. When deprived of special immunity he had, of course, no alternative but to speak.
    D. Having been obdurate until now, he was reluctant to surrender under this final pressure exerted upon him.

16. Select the sentence containing a predicate nominative. 16.____
    A. His dying wish, which he expressed almost with his last breath, was to see that justice was done toward his estranged wife.
    B. So long as we continue to elect our officials in truly democratic fashion, we shall have the power to preserve our liberties.
    C. We could do nothing, at this juncture, but walk the five miles back to camp.
    D. There was the spaniel, wet and cold and miserable, waiting silently at the door.

17. Select the sentence containing exactly TWO adverbs. 17.____
    A. The gentlemen advanced with exasperating deliberateness, while his lonely partner waited.
    B. If you are well, will you come early?
    C. I think you have guessed right, though you were rather slow, I must say.
    D. The last hundred years have seen more change than a thousand years of the Roman Empire, than a hundred thousand years of the stone age.

Questions 18-24.

DIRECTIONS: Select the choice describing the error in the sentence.

18. If us seniors do not support school functions, who will?
    A. Unnecessary shift in tense
    B. Incomplete sentence
    C. Improper case of pronoun
    D. Lack of parallelism

19. The principal has issued regulations which, in my opinion, I think are too harsh.
    A. Incorrect punctuation
    B. Faulty sentence structure
    C. Misspelling
    D. Redundant expression

20. The freshmens' and sophomores' performances equaled those of the juniors and seniors.
    A. Ambiguous reference
    B. Incorrect placement of punctuation
    C. Misspelling of past tense
    D. Incomplete comparison

21. Each of them, Anne and her, is an outstanding pianist I can't tell you which one is best.
    A. Lack of agreement
    B. Improper degree of comparison
    C. Incorrect case of pronoun
    D. Run-on sentence

22. She wears clothes that are more expensive than my other friends.
    A. Misuse of *than*
    B. Incorrect relative pronoun
    C. Shift in tense
    D. Faulty comparison

23. At the very end of the story it implies that the children's father died tragically.
    A. Misuse of *implies*
    B. Indefinite use of pronoun
    C. Incorrect spelling
    D. Incorrect possessive

24. At the end of the game both of us, John and me, couldn't scarcely walk because we were so tired.
    A. Incorrect punctuation
    B. Run-on sentence
    C. Incorrect case of pronoun
    D. Double negative

Questions 25-30.

DIRECTIONS: Questions 25 through 30 consist of a sentence lacking certain needed punctuation. Pick as your answer the description of punctuation which will CORRECTLY complete the sentence.

25. If you take the time to keep up your daily correspondence you will no doubt be most efficient.
    A. Comma only after *doubt*
    B. Comma only after *correspondence*
    C. Commas after *correspondence*, *will*, and *be*
    D. Commas after *if*, *correspondence*, and *will*

5 (#2)

26. Because he did not send the application soon enough he did not receive the
up to date copy of the book.
    A. Commas after *application* and *enough, and quotation marks before* up *and after* date
    B. Commas after *application* and *enough*, and hyphens between *to* and *date*
    C. Comma after *enough*, and hyphens between *up* and *to* and between *to* and *date*
    D. Comma after *application*, and quotation marks before *up* and after *date*

26.____

27. The coordinator requested from the department the following items a letter each
week summarizing progress personal forms and completed applications for tests.
    A. Commas after *items* and *completed*
    B. Semi-colon after *items* and *progress*, comma after *forms*
    C. Colon after *items*, commas after *progress* and *forms*
    D. Colon after *items*, commas after *forms* and *applications*

27.____

28. The supervisor asked Who will attend the conference next month.
    A. Comma after *asked*, period after *month*
    B. Period after *asked*, question mark after *month*
    C. Comma after *asked*, quotation marks before *Who*, quotation marks after *month*, and question mark after the quotation marks
    D. Comma after *asked*, quotation marks before *Who*, question mark after *month*, and quotation marks after the question mark

28.____

29. When the statistics are collected, we will forward the results to you as soon as
possible.
    A. Comma after *you*
    B. Commas after *forward* and *you*
    C. Commas after *collected, results* and *you*
    D. Comma after *collected*

29.____

30. The ecology of our environment is concerned with mans pollution of the
atmosphere.
    A. Comma after *ecology*
    B. Apostrophe after *n* and before *s* in *mans*
    C. Commas after *ecology* and *environment*
    D. Apostrophe after *s* in *mans*

30.____

KEY (CORRECT ANSWERS)

1.	D	11.	C	21.	B
2.	A	12.	D	22.	D
3.	D	13.	B	23.	B
4.	A	14.	A	24.	D
5.	B	15.	A	25.	B
6.	D	16.	A	26.	C
7.	A	17.	C	27.	C
8.	C	18.	C	28.	D
9.	A	19.	D	29.	D
10.	A	20.	B	30.	B

TEST 3

DIRECTIONS: Each question or incomplete statement is followed by several suggested answers or completions. Select the one that BEST answers the question or completes the statement. *PRINT THE LETTER OF THE CORRECT ANSWER IN THE SPACE AT THE RIGHT.*

Questions 1-6.

DIRECTIONS: From the four choices offered in Questions 1 through 6, select the one which is INCORRECT.

1. A. Before we try to extricate ourselves from this struggle in which we are now engaged in, we must be sure that we are not severing ties of honor and duty.
   B. Besides being an outstanding student, he is also a leader in school government and a trophy-winner in school sports.
   C. If the framers of the Constitution were to return to life for a day, their opinion of our amendments would be interesting.
   D. Since there are three m's in the word, it is frequently misspelled.

1.____

2. A. It was a college with an excellance beyond question.
   B. The coach will accompany the winners, whomever they may be.
   C. The dean, together with some other faculty members, is planning a conference.
   D. The jury are arguing among themselves.

2.____

3. A. This box is less nearly square than that one.
   B. Wagner is many persons' choice as the world's greatest composer.
   C. The habits of Copperheads are different from Diamond Backs.
   D. The teacher maintains that the child was insolent.

3.____

4. A. There was a time when the Far North was unknown territory. Now American soldiers manning radar stations there wave to Boeing jet planes zooming by overhead.
   B. Exodus, the psalms, and Deuteronomy are all books of the Old Testament.
   C. Linda identified her china dishes by marking their bottoms with india ink.
   D. Harry S. Truman, former president of the United States, served as a captain in the American army during World War I.

4.____

5. A. The sequel of their marriage was a divorce.
   B. We bought our car secondhand.
   C. His whereabouts is unknown.
   D. Jones offered to use his own car, providing the company would pay for gasoline, oil, and repairs,

5.____

6. A. I read Golding's "Lord of the Flies".
    B. The orator at the civil rights rally thrilled the audience when he said, "I quote Robert Burns's line, 'A man's a man for a' that."
    C. The phrase "producer to consumer" is commonly used by market analysts.
    D. The lawyer shouted, "Is not this evidence illegal?"

Questions 7-9.

DIRECTIONS: In answering Questions 7 through 9, mark the letter A if faulty because of incorrect grammar, mark the letter B if faulty because of incorrect punctuation, mark the letter C if correct.

7. Mr. Brown our accountant, will audit the accounts next week.

8. Give the assignment to whomever is able to do it most efficiently.

9. The supervisor expected either your or I to file these reports.

Questions 10-14.

DIRECTIONS: In each of the following groups of four sentences, one sentence contains an error in sentence structure, grammar, usage, diction, or punctuation. Indicate the INCORRECT sentence.

10. A. The agent asked, "Did you say, 'Never again?'"
    B. Kindly let me know whether you can visit us on the 17th.
    C. "I cannot accept that!" he exploded. "Please show me something else.
    D. Ed, will you please lend me your grass shears for an hour or so.

11. A. Recalcitrant though he may have been, Alexander was willfully destructive.
    B. Everybody should look out for himself.
    C. John is one of those students who usually spends most of his time in the principal's office.
    D. She seems to feel that what is theirs is hers.

12. A. Be he ever so much in the wrong, I'll support the man while deploring his actions.
    B. The schools' lack of interest in consumer education is shortsighted.
    C. I think that Fitzgerald's finest stanza is one which includes the reference to youth's "sweet-scented manuscript.
    D. I never would agree to Anderson having full control of the company's policies.

13. A. We had to walk about five miles before finding a gas station.
    B. The willful sending of a false alarm has, and may, result in homicide.
    C. Please bring that book to me at once.
    D. Neither my sister nor I am interested in bowling.

14. A. He is one of the very few football players who doesn't wear a helmet with a face guard.
    B. But three volunteers appeared at the recruiting office.
    C. Such consideration as you can give us will be appreciated.
    D. When I left them, the group were disagreeing about the proposed legislation.

Question 15.

DIRECTIONS: Question 15 contains two sentences concerning criminal law. The sentences could contain errors in English grammar or usage. A sentence does not contain an error simply because it could be written in a different manner. In answering this question, choose answer
A. if only sentence I is correct
B. if only sentence II is correct
C. if both sentences are correct
D. if neither sentence is correct

15. I. The use of fire or explosives to destroy tangible property is proscribed by the criminal mischief provisions of the Revised Penal Law.
    II. The defendant's taking of a taxicab for the immediate purpose of affecting his escape did not constitute grand larceny.

KEY (CORRECT ANSWERS)

1.	A	6.	A	11.	C
2.	B	7.	B	12.	D
3.	C	8.	A	13.	B
4.	B	9.	A	14.	A
5.	D	10	A	15.	A

BASIC FUNDAMENTALS OF VITAMINS

I. WHAT ARE VITAMINS?

They are a group of organic (carbon-containing) compounds that regulate reactions occurring in metabolism — the process by which the body breaks down and uses foods. Once called accessory food factors, vitamins are necessary because, just as water needs heat to boil, certain processes in the body won't occur properly without vitamins. Scientists don't fully understand why. The most popular theory is that the vitamins serve as traffic controllers, telling the body when certain procedures may begin, or determining speed and duration. Thus, the absence of a vitamin may block a reaction in a cell, thereby disrupting the cell's balance and causing it to form improperly or function abnormally.

Unlike some other organisms, the human body does not manufacture vitamins, and needs to acquire them from diet. Scientists now think that the reason is built in, a result of evolution. In the beginning, the theory goes, simple organisms could get everything they needed straight from the environment. But as life forms became more complex, the ability to make those compounds directly from elements in nature was lost. And in the case of vitamin C, they think that our body's inability to synthesize it is a form of *genetic disease*. That is, we did not discard the ability on the way to becoming *man*, but rather something went wrong in the formation of our metabolic process so that the ingredients we need to make vitamin C are completely missing.

Vitamins are subdivided into two basic classifications — water-soluble and fat-soluble.

Water-soluble vitamins (except vitamin C) serve as catalysts in metabolic activity. They help the body transfer energy from food, and aid in breaking down fats, carbohydrates, and proteins. During digestion, those vitamins are absorbed into the intestine - where no chemical reaction is needed to make them usable - and then pass directly to the bloodstream, where they are carried to body tissues for use. Each of the water-soluble vitamins serves a very special function in the body. For example, vitamins B_1 and B_6 control the conversion of carbohydrates and proteins into metabolic energy (calories), while niacin and riboflavin transport hydrogen during metabolism, thereby causing specific proteins, fats, and carbohydrates to be formed. Vitamin C aids in the formation of collagen, the connective tissue of skin, tendons, and bone, and in absorption and use of iron and potassium. Water-soluble vitamins are not normally stored in the body.

The fat-soluble vitamins are a much more sophisticated group. They serve more highly specialized functions and are much more selectively distributed in nature. They include vitamins A, D, E, and K, all of which can be stored in the body and can be toxic when taken in excess. The fat-solubles are necessary for the synthesis of some body enzymes (substances that speed up or start chemical reactions in the body), and form part of many biological membranes. They are transported by lymph from the intestines to the circulating blood. More fat-solubles than water-solubles are stored in the body, with A, D, and K stored in the liver and vitamin E stored in body fat. Also, since fat is necessary to break down those vitamins, anything that impedes fat metabolism can inhibit their use.

One of the best ways to make sure that your diet is providing your body with what it needs is to make sure that it is varied. It doesn't really matter if you do not savor a few members of any of the basic food groups, since there are enough other foods rich in the same nutrients to take up the slack. You don't have to eat liver to get iron, if you dislike it. Eat spinach in a salad instead and get plenty of iron and some vitamin A too.

Contrary to the faddist notion, the idea of taking each little vitamin in a separate tablet (as opposed to the more common multiple-vitamin tablet) is wrong. What people are doing by this practice is spending a good deal of money and taking the chance of vitamin overdose. It is simply useless to load the body with substances it can't possibly utilize.

In fact, the whole idea of vitamin pills is superfluous unless a person (1) has an illness that eliminates an entire food group from the diet, (2) is the sort of vegetarian who eschews eggs, butter, milk, cheese, and all meats, poultry, and fish, or (3) is pregnant, sick or so poor that a varied, quality diet is impossible. If you are in doubt about your supply of vitamins, ask your physician for advice and take only those prescribed.

Also, people should interpret in a common-sense way the *recommended daily requirement* phrase. This simply refers to an optimum amount that scientists have found to be healthy for humans. One will find that the United States requires one amount, Canada another, and some other country another. This doesn't at all mean that, if you're getting less than this amount of a vitamin, you're deficient.

II. FAT-SOLUBLE VITAMINS

Vitamin	Uses	Possible Results of Deficiency	Possible Results of Surplus	Sources
A (Retinol)	Serves in the formation of normal skin and the mucosa, internal skin, bone, and tooth formation, night and color vision	Deterioration of skin, faulty bone and tooth development, deterioration of eyes, night blindness and blindness	Drying and peeling of skin, loss of hair, bone, and joint pain, fragile bones, enlarged liver and spleen; in severe cases, death	Liver, butter, and fortified margarine, cream, whole milk and cheese made from whole milk, carrots, and dark green leafy vegetables
D	Regulates intestinal absorption of calcium and phosphorus and utilization of those minerals in bones and soft tissue, and plays a part in protein metabolism	In children: delayed tooth development, large joints, soft bones that are easily deformed and broken, deformities of chest, skull, spine, and pelvis (rickets). In adults: osteo-malacia (adult rickets), characterized by softening of bones	Weakness, weight loss, vomiting, diarrhea, calcium deposits in soft tissues, kidney damage and death	Formed by direct exposure of skin to sunlight, fortified milk, fish liver oils; also, small amounts of butter made in the summer, liver, egg yolk, and fatty fish like sardines, salmon, and tuna

Vitamin	Uses	Possible Results of Deficiency	Possible Results of Surplus	Sources
E	An antioxidant to reduce oxidation of vitamin A, the carotenes, and polyunsaturated fatty acids	Deficiency (rare and even difficult to produce experimentally) causes mild anemia and destruction of red blood cells	Excess (although there is no conclusive evidence) is believed to cause muscle damage and fatigue	Vegetable oils like cottonseed, safflower, sunflower, soybean; corn, almonds, peanuts, wheat germ, rice germ, asparagus, green leafy vegetables, liver, margarine, vegetable shortening
K	Necessary for proper clotting of blood	Leads to prolonged clotting time and hemorrhagic disease in newborn infants	Excess of menaquinone, a synthetic form, can cause jaundice in newborn infants, but natural forms have not been found to be toxic. An excess in adults is unlikely.	The main source is synthesis by normal bacteria in the intestine, a function that can be inhibited by some antibiotics. Food sources include lettuce, spinach, kale, cauliflower, cabbage, liver, egg yolk, soybean oils.

III. WATER-SOLUBLE VITAMINS

Vitamin	Uses	Possible Results of Deficiency	Possible Results of Surplus	Sources
C (Ascorbic Acid)	Aids in the formation of collagen, the connective tissue of skin, tendons, and bone, in the formation of hemoglobin, the absorption and use of iron and phosphorus, and possibly in the metabolism of protein and carbohydrates.	Poor bone and tooth development, bleeding gums, weakened cartilage and capillary walls, skin hemorrhages, anemia (scurvy)	A possible factor in the destruction of vitamin B_{12} in ingested food.	Citrus fruits, tomatoes, cantaloupe, and other melons, berries, green leafy vegetables, peppers, broccoli, cauliflower, and fresh potatoes

Vitamin	Uses	Possible Results of Deficiency	Possible Results of Surplus	Sources
B_1 (Thiamine)	Necessary for carbohydrate metabolism	Apathy, depression, poor appetite, lack of tone in the gastrointestinal tract, constipation, heart failure (beriberi)	No known effects	Whole-grain flours and cereals, wheat germ, seeds like sunflower and sesame, nuts like peanuts and pine nuts, legumes like soybeans, organ meats, pork (one of the richest sources) and leafy vegetables
B_2 (Riboflavin)	Used in enzymes that transport hydrogen in the body as part of the metabolism of carbohydrates, fats, and proteins	Cracks at corners of lips, scaly skin around nose and ears, sore tongue and mouth, itching, burning eyes, sensitivity to light	No known effects	Liver, kidney, cheese, milk, eggs, leafy vegetables, enriched bread, lean meat, beans, and peas
Niacin	Forms part of coenzymes needed for hydrogen transport and for health of tissue cells	Skin rash, sore mouth and tongue, inflamed membranes in the digestive tract, depression, mental disorientation and stupor (pellagra)	Flushing of skin and occasionally jaundice	Organ meats, lean meats, poultry, fish, wheat germ and whole-grain flours and cereals, nuts, seeds, rice, beans, and peas. The amino acid tryptophan can be converted to niacin in the body
B_6	Used in metabolism of protein, essential for conversion of the amino acid tryptophan to niacin in the body	Dermatitis around eyes, at angles of mouth, sore mouth and smooth red tongue, weight loss, dizziness, vomiting, anemia, kidney stones, nervous disturbances and convulsions	No known effects	Seeds like sunflower, wheat germ and bran, whole-grain bread, flours and cereals, liver, meats, fish and poultry, potatoes, beans and brown rice

Vitamin	Uses	Possible Results of Deficiency	Possible Results of Surplus	Sources
Pantothenic acid	Essential to many chemical reactions, particularly metabolism and release of energy from fat, protein, and carbohydrates	Unlikely unless a part of total B vitamin deficiency. Unless the diet consists solely of highly processed foods, this deficiency is seldom seen	No known effects	Liver, eggs, wheat germ, peanuts, and peas; widely distributed in most foods
Biotin	Essential for metabolism of protein, fats, and carbohydrates and energy release	Dermatitis, loss of appetite, nausea, insomnia, deep depression, and muscle pain. Occurs only when large quantities of raw egg whites are consumed over a long period since audin, a protein in raw egg white, blocks absorption of biotin	No known effects	Widely distributed in food, but the best sources are liver, egg yolk, nuts, and legumes
Folic Acid	Essential for the synthesis of nucleic acids, the building blocks life	Smooth red tongue, intestinal distress, macrocytic of anemia and failure of young red blood cells to mature	No known effects	Liver, leafy vegetables, dried beans and peas, asparagus and broccoli, fresh oranges, whole wheat flours, breads, and cereals
B_{12}	Synthesis of nucleic acids and the amino acid, aspartic acid	Sore tongue, weakness, weight loss, tingling hands and feet, back pain, mental and nervous changes, eventually pernicious anemia, and irreversible deterioration of the spinal cord	No known effects	Only in animal foods like liver, meats, poultry, fish, and shellfish, eggs and milk and milk products

Glossary of Dietary Terms

CONTENTS

	Page
Absorption .... Available	1
Avidin ....Carbohydrate	2
Carob powder .... Denaturation	3
Dixtrin ....Exchange list	4
Excipient ....Hyperkalemia	5
Hyperlipoproteinemia ....Lactose intolerance	6
Lecithin ....Mineral oil	7
Monosaccharides ....Pasteurized	8
Pellagra ....Saccharin	9
Salt ....Urea	10
Uremia ....Zinc	11

Glossary of Dietary Terms

Absorption. Assimilation or taking up of nutrients, fluids, gases, or other substances by the stomach or intestinal walls following digestion.

Acetone (dimethyl ketone). Product of incomplete oxidation of fats. May occur in diabetes mellitus, giving a fruity odor to the breath.

Acid-forming foods. Foods in which the acidic residue exceeds the alkaline residue.

Acidosis. An abnormal increase of acids in the blood caused by accumulation of an excess of acids in the body or by excessive loss of base; characterized by a fall in the pH of the blood or decrease in the alkali reserve in the body. Examples of acidosis include the ketosis (of diabetes mellitus), phosphoric, sulfuric, and hydrochloric acids (of renal insufficiency), lactic acid (or prolonged exercise), and carbonic acid (in respiratory disease).

ADA. Abbreviation for the American Dietetic Association, American Diabetes Association, and American Dental Association.

Adipose. Fat or fatty.

Alcohol. Ethanol. Ethyl alcohol. Distilled from the products of anaerobic fermentation of carbohydrate. An ingredient in a variety of beverages including beer, wine, liqueurs, cordials, and mixed or straight drinks. Pure alcohol itself yields about seven Calories per gram, of which more than 75 percent is available to the body.

Alkaline-forming foods. Foods in which the alkaline residue exceeds the acidic residue.

Alkalosis. An excess of base in the body, commonly resulting from persistent vomiting, excessive sodium bicarbonate intake, or hyperventilation. An abnormal condition of elevated blood pH caused by excessive loss of acids from the body without comparable loss of base or more supply of base than can be neutralized or eliminated.

Allergen. Any agent or substance (usually protein) capable of producing an allergic reaction.

Amino acid (AA). Chief components of proteins. Each amino acid molecule contains one or more amino group (— NH_2) and carboxyl group (— COOH). Amino acids may be acid, basic, or neutral.

Anabolism. Process of building simple substances into more complex substances.

Anemia. Deficiency in the circulating hemoglobin, red blood cells, or packed cell volume resulting in decreased capacity of the blood to carry oxygen. Macrocytic (large cell size) anemias may result from folacin and B_{12} deficiencies. Microcytic (small cell size), hypochromic (low color index) anemia may result from iron deficiency. Iron, protein, folic acid, vitamin B_{12}, and vitamin C are the major nutrients essential in blood formation.

Anorexia. Lack or loss of appetite for food.

Antibiotic. A substance that destroys or inhibits the growth of bacteria and other micro-organisms.

Antioxidant. A substance which delays or prevents oxidation.

Antivitamin. A substance which may inactivate or destroy a vitamin.

Anuria. Suppression or absence of urinary excretion.

Apatite. Complex calcium phosphate salt giving strength to bones.

Appetite. Natural desire or craving for food.

Arteriosclerosis. Hardening, thickening, and loss of elasticity of the inner walls of arteries and capillaries.

Artificial sweeteners. See saccharin, sorbitol, mannitol, and cyclamate.

Ascorbic acid. Reduced form of vitamin C; water soluble vitamin; prevents scurvy.

Ash. Mineral residue remaining after burning or oxidizing all organic matter.

As Purchased (AP). The weight of food before removing or trimming inedible parts.

Atherosclerosis. A fatty degeneration of the blood vessels and connective tissue of arterial walls. A kind of arteriosclerosis. The fatty deposits, including cholesterol, phospholipids, triglycerides, and other substances, decrease the internal channel size of the blood vessel.

Atony. Lack of normal tone or strength.

Atrophy. A wasting away of the cell, tissue, or organ.

Available. A nutrient that is in a form readily

absorbed by the digestive tract and usable by the body.

Avidin. A protein in raw egg white which binds with the B vitamin, biotin, and prevents its absorption from the digestive tract. Cooking inactivates avidin.

Avitaminosis. A condition due to inadequate vitamin intake or absorption, increased body require. ment, or antivitamins.

Azotemia uremia. Retention of urea or other nitrogenous substances in the urine.

Balance study. Quantitative method of measuring amount of a nutrient ingested and excreted to determine retention (positive balance) or loss (negative balance).

Basal metabolism. Energy expended at complete physical and mental rest (12-to-16 hours after food ingestion and in thermally neutral temperature). Includes energy for respiration, circulation, gastrointestinal contractions, muscle tone, body temperature, and organ function. Basal metabolic rate (BMR) for an adult is approximately one Calorie per kilogram body weight per hour.

Beikost. Foods other than milk or formula.

Beriberi. Nutritional deficiency of thiamin (vitamin B_1) resulting in loss of appetite, general weakness, progressive edema, polyneuritis, and enlarged heart.

Bile. A fluid produced in the liver, stored, and concentrated in the gallbladder, and emptied into the duodenum to aid in digestion of fat.

Biological value (BV). The efficiency of food protein in supplying amino acids in the proper amounts for protein synthesis in the body. For example, meat has a high biological value (HBV) and beans have a low value. The Thomas-Mitchell equation for calculating BV follows:

$$\%BV = \frac{100\% \times N \text{ intake} - [(FN - MN) + (UN - EN)]}{N \text{ intake} - (FN - MN)}$$

where N = nitrogen, FN = fecal nitrogen, MN = metabolic nitrogen, UN = urinary nitrogen, and EN = endogenous nitrogen.

Biotin. A member of the water-soluble vitamin B complex; aids in fixation of carbon dioxide in fatty acid synthesis. Widely distributed in foodstuffs and synthesized by intestinal bacteria. Deficiency may be induced by large amount of avidin, causing scaly dermatitis, muscle pains, general malaise, and depression.

Bland. Any food that is not irritating to the gastric mucosa.

Blood lipids. Primarily cholesterol, phospholipid, and triglyceride which are bound to protein and circulate in the plasma.

Blood sugar level (BSL). The level of glucose (blood sugar) per 100 ml blood.

Bowel. The intestines.

Bran. The outer layer of whole grain. It contains iron, phosphorus, B vitamins, and fiber. Fiber absorbs water, softens and increases the bulk of stools, and facilitates elimination.

Brat diet. Diet consisting of banana, rice, applesauce, and toast; prescribed for diarrhea, especially for infants and children.

Bulk. The indigestible portion of carbohydrates which cannot he hydrolyzed by gastrointestinal enzymes.

Bulking agent. A metabolically inert substance which increases food volume without increasing calories.

BUN. Blood urea nitrogen.

Caffeine. An alkaloidal purine in coffee, tea, and cola drinks. A cardiac and renal stimulant which produces varying pharmacologic responses.

Calciferol. Vitamin D_2. A fat soluble vitamin produced by ergosterol irradiation. Prevents rickets.

Calcium. A major mineral, essential in bone formation, blood clotting, muscle tone, and nerve function. Deficiency may result in rickets or possibly osteomalacia.

Caffeine. An alkaloidal purine in coffee, tea, and cola drinks. A cardiac and renal stimulant which produces varying pharmacologic responses.

Calciferol. Vitamin D2. A fat soluble vitamin produced by ergosterol irradiation. Prevents rickets.

Calcium. A major mineral, essential in bone formation, blood clotting, muscle tone, and nerve function. Deficiency may result in rickets or possibly osteomalacia.

Calorie. The amount of heat energy required to raise the temperature of one kilogram of water one degree Centigrade. This is the large Calorie, or kilocalorie as used in nutrition. Calories come from carbohydrate, protein, fat, alcohol, and alcohol derivatives (like sorbitol).

Calculus. Commonly called stone.

Carbohydrate. One of three major energy sources in food. Contains carbon, hydrogen, and oxygen. *Available carbohydrates*, such as sugar and starch, provide glucose and glycogen to the body and supply four Calories per gram. *Indigestible carbohydrate* is primarily indigestible plant cellulose.

Carob powder. A powder that looks and tastes like chocolate but does not contain lactose. It may be used as a substitute for chocolate on lactose and galactose restricted diets.

Carotene. Yellow-red plant pigment converted in the body to vitamin A. Two international units of betacarotene are equivalent to one international unit of vitamin A. Abundant in green leafy, and yellow vegetables.

Casein. A milk protein which can contain large amounts of lactose. A phosphoprotein.

Casein hydrolysate. Chemical decomposition of the principal protein of milk.

Catabolism. Opposite of anabolism. Metabolic process in which complex substances are broken down into simpler substances, usually yielding energy. Destructive metabolism.

Catecholamines. Chemicals synthesized in the brain, sympathetic nerve endings, peripheral tissues, and adrenal medulla.

Celiac disease. Malabsorptive syndrome due to sensitivity to gluten and resulting in decreased jejunal mucosa absorption of fat, carbohydrates, protein, vitamins, and minerals. See Wheat Elimination, paragraph 11-3.

Cellulose. The structural fibers in plants. Indigestible polysaccharide which provides bulk to the diet.

Cholecalciferol. Vitamin D_2. Initiates production of a calcium-binding protein.

Cholesterol. Fat-like steroid alcohol found in all tissues. It may be synthesized in the body, but is usually absorbed from the digestive tract in the presence of fat. It is excreted in bile. Foods of animal origin are dietary sources of cholesterol. It is a key part of the fatty deposits in the arterial wall in atherosclerosis.

Choline. A component of lecithin. Necessary for fat transport, preventing accumulation of fat in the liver. Occurs in all plant and animal cells and may be synthesized from glycine (an amino acid) in the presence of a methyl group.

Chylomicron. A blood lipoprotein containing primarily triglycerides from dietary fat and smaller amounts of cholesterol, phospholipid, and protein.

Chyluria. The presence of a fat globule emulsion, formed in the small intestine after digestion, in the urine giving it a milky appearance.

Clinical nutrition. That branch of the health sciences having to do with the diagnosis, treatment, and prevention of human disease caused by deficiency, excess, or metabolic imbalance of dietary nutrients.

Cobalamin. Vitamin B_{12}. Antipernicious anemia factor; extrinsic factor.

Coffee oils. Possible cause of gastrointestinal irritation, diarrhea is a common symptom.

Colloid. A material whose particles are between 1 and 100 millimicrons in size and dispersed throughout a medium. The particles in dispersion are larger than ordinary crystalloid molecules but are not large enough to settle out under the influence of gravity. Examples are blood protein and gelatin.

Connective tissue. Collagen and elastin. Collagen is converted to gelatin by moist heat cookery. Elastin is not broken down or softened in cooking.

Creatinine. One of the end products of food protein breakdown. The amount excreted in the urine is an index of muscle mass and may be used as a measure of basal heat production. **Clear liquid dessert.** Desserts that provide little or no residue, including plain gelatin and Popsicles.

Crystalloid. Small molecules dissolved in a medium such as salt dissolved in water. Other examples are Na^+, K^+, other electrolytes, BUN, uric acid, and creatinine dissolved in the blood.

Curds. The clumped part of curdled milk which contains lactose.

Cyanocobalamin. Vitamin B_{12}.

Cyclamates. A noncaloric sweetener with 30 to 60 times the sweet taste of sucrose. A sodium or calcium salt of cyclohexylsulfamic acid. Cyclamate was changed from the GRAS (generally recognized as safe by the Food and Drug Administration) list to drug status, permitting use only under medical supervision. A suspected carcinogen.

Dehydration. Removal of water from food, tissue, or substrate.

Dehydroascorbic acid. Oxidized vitamin C; biologically active; reversibly oxidized and reduced. **Deciliter.** One-tenth of a liter.

Denaturation. To change the chemical,

physical, or biologic properties of protein by heating, freezing, irradiation, pressure, or organic solvent application.

Dextrin. The intermediate product of starch breakdown; a polysaccharide.

Dialysis. To separate substances in a solution by using a semipermeable membrane; small substances will pass through and larger molecules will not. As used in food preparation, see attachment 5.

Diet. Food and drink consumed. See specific types in text.

Dietary consultation. Individualized professional guidance provided to assist patients in adapting food consumption to meet health needs. The patient's background, socioeconomic needs, and personal preferences are considered when instructing patients on the physician-prescribed diet.

Dietary history. Record of an individual's food intake taken by 24-hour recall or repeated food records. Basis for individualized dietary consultation.

Dietary status. Bodily condition resulting from the utilization of the essential nutrients available to the body. Dietary history provides some indication of dietary status.

Dietetics. The science and art of planning, preparing, and serving meals to individuals and groups according to the principles of nutrition and management; economic, social, cultural, psychological, and health or disease conditions are considered.

Dietitian. A professional who practices dietetics after following a prescribed academic program for a baccalaureate degree in an accredited institution and completing an accredited internship, or equivalent.

Dietitian, Registered (R.D.). A qualified dietitian who has also successfully completed the examination for professional registration and maintains continuing education requirements by completing 75 clock hours of professional education every 5 years.

Digestibility. The amount of nutrient absorbed by the body and not excreted in the feces.

Digestion. Process of converting food into substances which can be absorbed by the body.

Disaccharidase. An enzyme which hydrolyzes disaccharides to yield two single sugars.

Diuresis. Increased secretion of urine.

Dumping syndrome. Postgastrectomy epigastric discomfort resulting when a large amount of hypertonic, concentrated food draws large quantities of fluid from the bloodstream into the intestine.

Duodenum. The first segment of small intestine between the pylorus and jejunum. Pancreatic juice and bile are secreted into the duodenum.

Edible portion (EP). The trimmed weight of food that is normally eaten.

Effusion. Fluid escaping into a part or tissue.

Endogenous. Originating within the cell or tissue.

Endogenous protein. Body or tissue protein.

Energy. Capacity to do work, such as muscular activity, maintaining body temperature, and operating metabolic processes. As obtained from food oxidation, energy is expressed in calories.

Enrichment. The addition of one or more nutrients to a food to attain a higher level of those nutrients than normally present in the food. Bread and flour are often enriched.

Enteral. Within or by way of the intestine. Often used to refer to supplemental oral, or tube feedings.

Enzyme. An organic compound (usually protein) which accelerates metabolic reactions (such as digestion).

Epinephrine. A hormone released primarily in response to hypoglycemia. It increases blood pressure, stimulates the heart muscle, accelerates the heart rate, and increases cardiac output.

Ergosterol. A plant steroid converted to vitamin D_2, calciferol, upon irradiation or exposure to ultraviolet light.

Essential amino acid. Those amino acids that cannot be synthesized by the body; they must be obtained from food to ensure normal growth, development, and tissue repair.

Essential fatty acid. Fatty acids that cannot be synthesized in adequate amounts by the body to ensure growth, reproduction, skin health, and proper fat utilization.

Ethanol. See alcohol.

Ethylenediamine-tetraacetate. A non-nutritive food additive used to separate a part from a whole, or to act as a metal scavenger.

Exchange list. Grouping of foods similar in nutrients together so they may be used interchangeably.

Excipient. Any addition to a medicine designed to permit proper shaping or consistency.

Exogenous. Originating outside, externally caused. Extrinsic factor. Vitamin B_{12}.

Exudative enteropathics. Any disease of the intestine with material escaped from the blood vessels deposited in the intestine.

Fat. One of three major sources of food energy, which provides nine Calories per gram. A mixture of glyceryl esters of fatty acids; an oily, yellow, or white substance of animal or vegetable sources.

Fatty acid. Organic acids which combine with glycerol to form fat.

Favism. An acute hemolytic anemia resulting from ingestion of fava beans (horse or broad beans).

Ferment. Chemical change caused by digestive enzymes of micro-organisms.

Fiber. An indigestible part of fruits, vegetables, cereals, and grains important in the diet as roughage, or bulk.

Flatulence. Excessive gas in the stomach or intestines.

Focacin. Folic acid. Pteroylglutamic acid. A water-soluble vitamin of the B complex group needed for normal growth and hemopoiesis. Widely distributed in plant and animal tissues. Deficiency may be induced by sulfonamides or folic acid antagonists.

Food habit. Usual pattern of an individual or group for choosing, preparing, and eating food resulting from family, cultural, economic, and religious influences.

Fortification. The addition of one or more nutrients to a food whether or not they are naturally present. An example is margarine fortified with vitamin A.

Full liquid dessert. Desserts that are fluid or that easily become fluid, including plain gelatin, ice cream, soft custard, and pudding.

Galactose. A six carbon monosaccharide.

Galactosemia. Galactose in the blood due to an inborn error of metabolism in which the enzyme galactose-l-phosphate uridyl transferase is absent; thus, galactose is not converted to glucose. Mental and growth retardation, liver and spleen enlargement, cataracts, jaundice, weight loss, vomiting, and diarrhea result unless dietary modification eliminates lactose-and galactose-containing foods from the diet.

Gavage. Feeding via insertion of a tube through the mouth into the stomach.

Gelatin. An incomplete protein obtained from partial hydrolysis of collagen.

Geriatrics. Study and treatment of diseases and problems occurring in old age.

Glomerular filtration rate (GFR). Milliliters of blood which pass through the kidney glomeruli in one minute; may be used to estimate kidney function.

Glucose. Dextrose. Grape sugar. Blood sugar. A monosaccharide which may be absorbed into the bloodstream and is the major source of energy for the brain and nervous tissues.

Glutathione. A tripeptide believed to assist sulfhydryl containing enzymes to stay in the reduced state essential for their activity.

Gluten. A cereal grain protein; gluten provides elasticity to bread dough.

Glycogen. A polysaccharide composed of glucose units. The main form of carbohydrate stored by man and animals in liver, muscles, and other tissues.

Gram. A unit of mass and weight in the metric system. An ounce is approximately 28 grams.

Gravidity. Pregnancy.

Hemicellulose. A largely indigestible plant polysaccharide that absorbs water. Pectin is a hemi-cellulose that may lower serum cholesterol.

Hemodialysis. Dialyzing blood to remove waste products.

Hepatosplenomegaly. Enlargement of both liver and spleen.

High biological value (HBV) protein. A protein readily digested, absorbed, and utilized by the body, such as the protein in eggs.

Homeostasis. Balance of the internal environment including fluid, pH, body temperature, blood sugar level, heart and pulse rates, and hormonal control.

Hydrogenated oil. Addition of molecular hydrogen to double bonds in unsaturated fatty acids creating saturated solid fat with reduced essential fatty acid biological value.

Hypercholesterolemia. Elevated blood cholesterol associated with cardiovascular diseases.

Hyperchylomicronemia. Elevation of chylomicron lipoproteins circulating in the blood.

Hyperkalemia. Increased potassium in the blood. Hyperlipidemia. An elevation of one or

more lipid constituents of the blood.
Hyperlipoproteinemia. Elevation of blood lipoproteins.
Hypernatremia. Excessive amount of sodium in the blood.
Idiopathic. Without known origin.
Ileum. The part of the small intestine between the jejunum and large intestine.
Inborn error of metabolism. A metabolic defect existing at birth due to missing genes.
Incomplete protein. A protein lacking one or more essential amino acids.
Ingestion. Eating or drinking; taking in.
Inorganic. Minerals that do not contain carbon.
Inositol. A water soluble alcohol found primarily in cereal grains which combines with phosphate to form phytic acid.
Instant cereal. Pregelatinized (precooked) cereal requiring addition of water before serving.
Insulin. A hormone secreted by the beta cells of the islets of Langerhans in the pancreas. It is essential to carbohydrate metabolism in the body. Exogenous insulin is injected by some diabetics to provide proper carbohydrate metabolism.
Insulin shock (or) reaction. Very low blood sugar level resulting from overdose of insulin. Symptoms include hunger, weakness, nervousness, double vision, shallow breathing, sweating, headache, dizziness, mental confusion, muscular twitching, convulsion, loss of consciousness, coma, and eventually death. Fruit juice or intravenous glucose are often used to counteract insulin reaction.
International unit. A measure of biologic activity of a nutrient.
Interpolate. To determine intermediate values in a series based on observed values or to introduce new material in a given subject.
Intrinsic factor. Chemical in gastric juice that facilitates vitamin B_{12} (extrinsic factor) absorption. Lack of intrinsic factor results in pernicious anemia.
Iodine. A trace mineral essential in regulating basal metabolism. Deficiency results in goiter.
Iodine number (or) value. The number of grams of iodine absorbed by 100 grams of fat. Indicates the amount of fatty acids and degree of unsaturation of a fat. The iodine number of saturated coconut oil is 10, and that of polyunsaturated safflower oil is 100.

Iodized salt. Table salt with one part sodium or potassium iodide per 5,000 to 10,000 parts sodium chloride.
Irradiation. Exposure to ultraviolet rays used for destroying microorganisms in food and converting provitamin D to active vitamin D.
Isocaloric. Containing an equal number of Calories.
Jejunum. The part of the small intestine between the duodenum and ileum.
Joule. A metric measure of energy equaling 4.184 Calories.
Junket. The precipitated protein of milk casein and fat.
Ketogenic-antiketogenic ratio. The ratio of the amount of ketogenic factors, such as fatty acids and ketogenic amino acids, to the amount of anti-ketogenic factors, such as carbohydrates, glucogenic amino acids, and the glycerol of fat.
Ketosis. An accumulation of ketone bodies (beta-hydroxybutyric acid, acetoacetic acid, and acetone) from incomplete fatty acid oxidation. Uncontrolled ketosis may result in acidosis.
Kosher foods. Foods prepared and served by Orthodox Judaism dietary laws which include: (1) milk and meat are not consumed at the same meal, (2) meat must be slaughtered in a special ordained manner and cleaned (koshered) by soaking in water, salting, and washing, (3) meat from cud-chewing, cloven-hooved animals (cows, sheep, goats) may be eaten, (4) finfish may be eaten. No pork or shellfish are eaten.
Kwashiorkor. Severe protein malnutrition in children resulting in retarded growth, anemia, edema, fatty liver, lack of pigment in the hair and skin, gastrointestinal disorders, muscle atrophy, and psychomotor wasting.
Labile. Unstable.
Lactase. Enzyme that splits lactose to glucose and galactose.
Lactate, lactic acid, lactalbumin. Substances related to lactose but which cannot be changed into galactose by the body.
Lacto-ovo-vegetarian. Person subsisting on grains, legumes, vegetables, fruits, milk, and eggs. Meat, poultry and fish are avoided.
Lactose. "Milk sugar." Disaccharide occurring in milk products. Contains one glucose and one galactose group.
Lactose intolerance. Lactose malabsorption due to lactase deficiency. Results in

diarrhea.

Lecithin. Phosphatidyl choline. A phospholipid containing glycerol, fatty acids, phosphoric acid, and choline. Involved in fat transport, lecithin is found in many cells, especially nerves. Lecithin synthesis in the body depends upon dietary intake of methyl groups or choline.

Leucine. An essential amino acid with ketogenic properties.

Licorice. Black flavoring extract containing glycyrrhizic acid which, in large amounts, can cause hypertension and hypokalemia.

Lignin. A constituent of crude fiber. An indigestible cellulose. With cellulose, the principal Part of the woody plants. Unlike cellulose, lignin can combine with bile to form insoluble complexes which are not absorbed.

Linoleic acid. Polyunsaturated essential fatty acid with 18 carbon atoms and two double bonds.

Linolenic acid. A nonessential polyunsaturated fatty acid with 18 carbon atoms and three double bonds.

Lipid. Fat or fat-like substances. Includes fatty acids, triglycerides, phosphatides (such as lecithin), terpenes, and steroids (such as cholesterol).

Lipoprotein. A compound consisting of a simple protein and lipid and involved in lipid transport. Types of lipoprotein circulating in the blood include chylomicrons, alpha lipoproteins (high density lipoproteins, HDL), prebeta lipoproteins (very low density lipoproteins, VLDL), and beta lipoprotein (low density lipoprotein, LDL). All are composed of phospholipid, triglyceride, cholesterol, and protein.

Long-chain fatty acid. Fatty acids containing 12 or more carbon atoms, such as stearic (18 carbon) and palmatic (16 carbon) acids.

Low sodium milk. Milk processed by ion-exchange process to remove approximately 90 percent of the naturally occurring sodium. Thiamin, riboflavin, and calcium are also decreased with an increase in potassium.

Lycine. An essential amino acid and the limiting amino acid in many cereal products.

Magnesium. An essential mineral. A cofactor in metabolism.

Malabsorption syndrome. A condition caused by failure of the body to absorb nutrients such as fats, calcium and other minerals, and vitamins. Examples include celiac disease, chronic pancrea-titis, sprue, cystic fibrosis, and carbohydrate intolerance.

Malnutrition. Lack or excess of absorbed nutrients resulting in impaired health status.

Manganese. An essential trace mineral.

Mannitol. A partially absorbed sugar alcohol with a sweet taste equal to sugar but with half the calories.

Maple syrup urine disease. Inborn error of metabolism treated with dietary restriction of leucine. isoleucine, and valine.

Marasmus. Severe protein-calorie malnutrition of infants and young children.

Medium chain fatty acid. Fatty acids containing 8 to 10 carbon atoms, such as caprylic (8 carbon) and capric (10 carbon) acids.

Medium chain triglyceride (MCT). A fat composed primarily of saturated fatty acids with 8 to 10 carbon atoms. A commercially prepared food product for persons not able to digest or absorb food fats and oils.

Menadione. A synthetic, vitamin K_2 is much more potent biologically than vitamin K.

Metabolism. Chemical changes in the body: anabolism and catabolism.

Methionine. An essential amino acid important in protein and fat, metabolism.

Methylcellulose. Indigestible polysaccharide which provides bulk and satiety without. calories.

Micronutrient. Nutrients present. in less than 0.005 percent of body weight, such as trace minerals. Also, nutrients present in very small amounts in food.

Microgram. A metric system unit of mass representing one one-millionth of a gram or one one-thousandth of a milligram.

Milk-alkali syndrome. Ingestion of large quantities of milk and alkalies resulting in hypercalcemia, calcium in soft tissues, vomiting, gastrointestinal bleeding, and high blood pressure.

Milliosmole. One thousandth of an osmole.

Mineral. Inorganic elements that build and repair body tissue or control body functions. The ones known to be essential to man are calcium, chlorine, chromium, cobalt, copper, fluorine, iodine, iron, magnesium, manganese, molybdenum, phosphorus, potassium, selenium, sodium, sulfur. and zinc.

Mineral oil. Liquid petroleum substance which is not absorbed by the gastrointestinal tract but interferes with absorption of fat soluble vitamins.

Monosaccharides. Carbohydrates composed of single simple sugars that cannot be hydrolyzed (broken) into smaller units. Examples are fructose, galactose, glucose, and ribose.

Monounsaturated fat. Fat that neither raises nor lowers blood cholesterol. Examples are olive oil and peanut oil.

Monounsaturated fatty acid. Fatty acids with only one unsaturated double bond.

Monosodium glutamate (MSG). A sodium-containing flavoring used in Asian cookery.

Nasogastric tube. Used in tube feeding; a tube inserted via the nose and esophagus into the stomach.

Nausea. Stomach discomfort with a tendency to vomit.

Negative nitrogen balance. Daily nitrogen excretion greater than nitrogen intake which may be brought about by fever, surgery, or burns.

Niacin. Nicotenic acid. A water-soluble B complex vitamin. Antipellagra factor. Necessary to cell respiration, carbohydrate and protein metabolism, and lipid synthesis; thus, requirement varies with caloric intake.

Niacin equivalent. The sum of nicotinic acid and niacin is the niacin equivalent. Sixty milligrams tryptophan may be converted to one milligram nicotinic acid.

Nicotinic acid. Niacin.

Nitrogen balance/equilibrium. An individual is in nitrogen balance when the nitrogen intake from food protein each day is approximately equal to the nitrogen loss in feces and urine.

Non-nutritive sweetener. A noncaloric synthetic sugar substitute. Examples are saccharine and cyclamate.

Norepinephrine. A hormone released primarily in response to hypotension to raise blood pressure.

Nutrient. Any chemical substance useful in nutrition for providing heat and energy, building and repairing tissues, and regulating life processes.

Nutrition. The study of food in relation to health. Combination of processes by which the body receives and uses the materials necessary for body functions, energy, growth, and tissue renewal.

Nutrition history. Laboratory and clinical findings, and a dietary history.

Nutritional status. The condition of the body resulting from consumption and utilization of nutrients.

Nutriture. Tissue nutrient balance of supply and demand.

Obesity. Fat. Body weight approximately 20 percent or more above desirable weight due to adiposity.

Oil. A lipid that is liquid at room temperature.

Oleic acid. An 18 carbon monounsaturated fatty acid abundant in fats and oils.

Oliguria. Decreased urinary output in relation to fluid intake.

Oral hypoglycemic agents. Orally administered compounds that stimulate beta cells in the islands of Langerhans of the pancreas to secrete endogenous insulin that reduces blood glucose in diabetics. Contraindicated for some patients.

Osmolality. A property of a solution which depends on the concentration of the solute per unit of solvent.

Osmolarity. A property of a solution which depends on the concentration of the solute per unit of total volume of solution.

Osmole. The standard unit of osmotic pressure. Overweight. Fat. Body weight approximately 10 to 20 percent above desirable weight due to adiposity.

Oxalate. Salt of oxalic acid. When combined in insoluble calcium salts. oxalate renders calcium unavailable for absorption.

Pancreatic juice. A digestive juice produced by the pancreas and secreted into the duodenum; contains enzymes involved in digestion of protein, carbohydrate. and fat.

Pantothenic acid. A water-soluble B complex vitamin that is part of coenzyme A. It is essential for growth. normal skin. nervous system development, and adrenal cortex function.

Papain. A proteolytic enzyme of papaya often used as a meat tenderizer.

Parenteral feeding. Food provided without use of the mouth and digestive tract, such as intravenous feeding.

Pasteurized. Heat treated to kill most pathogenic microorganisms. For example. pasteurized eggnog prevents the potential of salmonella infection from eggnog made with raw eggs.

Pellagra. Multiple B vitamin deficiency, notably

of niacin. Symptoms include dermatitis, diarrhea, dementia, and death.

Peristalsis. Alternate contraction and relaxation pf the gastrointestinal tract which moves contents toward the anus.

Pernicious anemia. Chronic macrocytic anemia due to B_{12} and intrinsic factor deficiency.

pH. A measure of acidity and alkalinity.

Phenylalanine. An essential amino that may be converted to tyrosine. It can be ketogenic, glycogenic, and participate in transamination.

Phenylketonuria (PKU). Inborn error in metabolism resulting in the lack of the enzyme phenylal-anine hydroxylase. Phenylalanine cannot be converted to tyrosine without this enzyme. The resultant high levels of phenylalanine result in permanent mental retardation and poor growth and development unless there is close dietary control of phenylalanine ingestion.

Phosphorus. An essential mineral.

Polysaccharide. A complex carbohydrate containing more than four monosaccharides. Examples are glycogen, starch, and cellulose.

Polyunsaturated fatty acids (PUFA). Fatty acids with more than one unsaturated bond in the molecule.

Polyunsaturated: saturated fatty acid ratio (P/S ratio). The relative amount of polyunsaturated linoleic acid to total saturated fatty acids.

Positive nitrogen balance. Nitrogen intake exceeds nitrogen output, such as during infancy and childhood (tissue anabolism).

Potassium. An essential mineral of the intracellular fluids.

Pressor agent. Any substance that raises blood pressure.

Protein. The primary structure of plant and animal bodies. It is composed of amino acids and is approximately 16 percent nitrogen. Protein provides four Calories per gram.

Protein hydrolysate. A mixture of "predigested protein" in the form of amino acids and polypep-tides. Used for oral or parenteral feeding in cases of impaired digestion, such as pancreatic diseases.

Protein calorie malnutrition. A condition of severe tissue wasting, subcutaneous fat loss, and dehydration caused by inadequate protein and calorie intake.

Protein quality. A complete protein contains all the essential amino acids for growth and life. A partial protein maintains life but not growth. An incomplete protein can support neither growth nor life. If two incomplete proteins each supply the limiting amino acid(s) of the other, together they may be capable of supporting growth and life.

Protein-sparing. Refers to calories supplied by carbohydrates and fat. These calories save protein from being "burned" as energy so it may be used for anabolism.

Provitamin. A substance related to a vitamin but with no vitamin activity until it is converted to the biologically active form.

P/S ratio. Ratio of polyunsaturated to saturated fatty acids.

Pureed. A food blenderized to a paste consistency. Most baby foods are pureed.

Purine. Nitrogenous compounds of dietary or endogenous origin catabolized to uric acid in the body.

Pyridoxine. An alcohol form of vitamin 136, a B complex vitamin.

Quick-cooking cereal/rice. Cereals and rice that have disodium phosphate added to reduce their preparation time.

Raffinose. Trisaccharide containing glucose, galactose, and fructose. It is found in beets, roots, underground stems, cottonseed meal, and molasses.

Recommended (Daily) Dietary Allowances (RDA). Suggested amounts of nutrients to provide when planning diets. Designed to maintain good nutrition in healthy persons of average build and activity in a temperature climate with a margin of safety 10 to 50 percent above normal dietary requirements.

Reconstitute. To restore to the normal state, usually by adding water.

Refuse. Inedible, discarded foodstuffs.

Residue. Amount of bulk remaining in the digestive tract after digestion and absorption.

Retinol. A vitamin A alcohol.

Retinol equivalent (RE). Unit expressing vitamin A activity. One RE = 1 u retinol, 6 u beta-carotene, and 12 u for other provitamin A carotenoids.

Riboflavin. Vitamin B_2. Heat stable, water soluble vitamin essential to the health of skin and eyes.

Rickets. Vitamin D deficiency or disturbance of calcium-phosphorus metabolism.

Saccharin. A noncaloric artificial sweetener 700 times sweeter than sugar.

Salt. Table salt; sodium chloride; NaCl.

Satiety. Sense of fullness or comfort; gratification of appetite.

Saturated fat. A fat with no double bonds; chemically satisfied. Often solid at room temperature and usually of animal origin. Examples are butter, lard, and steak fat.

Scurvy. Vitamin C deficiency disease resulting in swollen bleeding gums, hemorrhage of the skin and mucous membranes, and anemia.

Secretagogue. An agent that stimulates secretion.

Short-chain fatty acid. Those containing four to six carbon atoms, such as caproic (6 carbon) and butyric (4 carbon) acids. Yields only about 5 Calories per gram.

Skinfold measurement. Measurement of the thickness of skin at body sites where adipose is normally deposited. Measured with a caliper and compared against a standard chart, it provides an estimate of degree of fatness.

Sodium. An essential mineral important in extra-cellular body fluids and in regulating many body functions.

Soft. Any easily digested food that is soft in texture and provides no harsh fibers or connective tissue.

Sorbitol. A sugar alcohol apparently metabolized without insulin. It contains 4 calories per gram and can be converted to utilizable carbohydrate in the form of glucose. Excessive use may cause gastrointestinal discomfort and diarrhea.

Specific dynamic action. Increased metabolism from heat of digesting, absorbing, and metabolizing food. Approximately 30 percent for protein, 13 percent, for fat, and 4 to 5 percent for carbohydrate.

Standard of identity of foods. Standards established by a government agency, primarily the US Food and Drug Administration, to define quality and container fill for foods.

Stachyose. Tetrasaccharide containing glucose, fructose, and two molecules of galactose. It is found in tubers, peas, lima beans, and beets.

Starch. Plant storage form of carbohydrate (just as the animal storage form is glycogen). A complex polysaccharide. Food sources include breads, cereals, and starchy vegetables.

Sucrose. Table sugar. A disaccharide composed of glucose and fructose.

Sugar. Sucrose. A sweet, soluble carbohydrate that provides 4 Calories of energy per gram.

Sulphur. An essential mineral.

Supplement. A concentrated source of nutrients, such as vitamins or minerals.

Supplementary feeding. Food provided in addition to regular meals to increase nutrient intake.

Sweetening agent (or) sweeteners. Natural sweeteners, such as sugar, or synthetic sweeteners, such as saccharin.

Synthesis. Putting elements together to form a whole.

Tea tannin. Possible cause of constipation.

Textured vegetable protein. Vegetable protein that is flavored, colored, and textured to resemble meat and poultry products.

Theobromine. The alkaloidal stimulant in cocoa beans, tea leaves, and cola nuts that acts as a diuretic, arterial dilator, and myocardial stimulant.

Thiamin. Vitamin B_2, a B complex vitamin and part of a coenzyme important in carbohydrate metabolism. Prevents beriberi.

Threonine. An essential amino acid.

Tocopherols. An alcohol-like group of substances. Four forms have vitamin E activity.

Tofu. Soybean curd; usually available in oriental grocery stores.

Trace minerals. Minerals required by the body in minute amounts.

Triglyceride. A fat composed of a glycerol molecule with three fatty acids.

Tryptophane. An essential amino acid. May be converted to niacin, and a source of the vasoconstrictor serotonin.

Tyramine. A decarboxylation product of tyrosine found in fermented cheeses, wines, and other foods. Produces severe hypertensive reaction if consumed in conjunction with monoamine oxidase inhibitory drugs.

Underweight. Body weight 10 percent or more below the established standards.

Unsaturated fatty acids. Those with one or more double bonds. Abundant in vegetable oils.

Urea. Major nitrogen containing product of protein metabolism and chief nitrogenous constituent of the urine.

Uremia. A toxic condition caused by the retention in the blood of urinary constituents including urea, creatine, uric acid, and other end products of protein metabolism.

Vasopressor. Any agent that causes contraction of the muscular tissue lining the arteries and capillaries.

Vegetarian (or) vegan. Person subsisting entirely or in a large part on fruits, grains, legumes, and vegetables. If eggs, fish, meat, milk, and poultry are totally excluded, a vegetarian diet may be deficient in calcium, phosphorus, riboflavin, and vitamins B_{12} and D. Pure vegetarian diets are usually inadequate in protein for children.

Viosterol. Vitamin D_2, a product of ergosterol irradiation.

Vitamin. Organic substance provided in minute amounts in food or endogenuously synthesized. Essential in metabolic functions.

Vitamin A. Fat-soluble vitamin necessary for normal skin and bone development, maintenance of vision, and synthesis of mucopolysaccharides.

Vitamin B complex. Water soluble vitamins often found together in nature. Vitamins B_1 (thiamin), B_2 (riboflavin), B_6 group (pyridoxine, pyridoxal, and pyridoxamine), B_{12} group (cobalamins), nicotinic acid (niacin), pteroylglutamic acid (PGA, folacin, or folic acid), pantothenic acid, and biotin. All except B_{12} are coenzymes.

Vitamin C. Water-soluble vitamin. Ascorbic acid.

Vitamin D. Fat-soluble vitamins including ergocalciferol (D_2) and cholecalciferol (D_3).

Vitamin E. Fat-soluble vitamin. Tocopherols.

Vitamin K. Fat-soluble vitamin consumed in food and produced endogenously by intestinal flora. Necessary for blood clotting.

Water. A major nutrient required by the body. Endogenous water is provided as a byproduct of metabolism. Exogenous water may be in the fluid form or contained in food.

Water requirement. Water functions by removing body heat and urinary excreta. One milliliter water per calorie is usually sufficient unless there is a pathological condition such as fever or burn.

Whey. A clear, watery liquid remaining when milk curdles. It contains lactose, but little or no fat.

Zanthine. Weakly basic alkaloid chemicals including caffeine, theophylline, and theobromine.

Zinc. An essential trace mineral involved in growth, digestion, and metabolism. Deficiency results in retarded growth, delayed sexual maturity, and delayed wound healing.

www.ingramcontent.com/pod-product-compliance
Lightning Source LLC
Chambersburg PA
CBHW082046300426
44117CB00015B/2631